DYNAMIC
POSITIONING
QUESTIONS & ANSWERS

DR SURENDER KUMAR

Notion Press

No.8, 3rd Cross Street
CIT Colony, Mylapore
Chennai, Tamil Nadu – 600004

First Published by Notion Press 2020
Copyright © Dr Surender Kumar 2020
All Rights Reserved.

ISBN 978-1-63633-634-3

CONTENTS

FOREWORD

I am personally very happy to write this foreword for this very special book on dynamic positioning questions and answers, authored by Dr Kumar.

We have a long association with Dr Kumar from the days when he was the Principal of Sir Derek Bibby Maritime Training Centre in Mumbai. The team was pioneer in introducing DP training in India. I personally know him from his days at Bibby training centre when we developed our association. I was happy to note that his efforts as a DP trainer were recognised when he was awarded the best trainer for the offshore courses in 2018. Dr Kumar is currently employed with Azureus Simulators Asia as Research and Development Advisor.

Dr Kumar has more than a decade's experience teaching maritime professionals in India, Nigeria, South Africa, Dubai, Korea Maritime and Oceans University, Busan, South Korea and Indonesia. He is truly an international maritime and DP trainer. His vast experience teaching DP to international students inspired him to write this book catering to the needs of the DP professionals.

The questions and answers format of the book makes it really interesting for the reader to learn the subject. For the benefit of Indonesian DP professionals, the book is being translated in Bahasa Indonesia. The idea of translating this to Bahasa

Indonesia was developed while interacting with numerous students while imparting DP training to both the prospective DP operators and the DP engineers in Azureus Offshore Training Centre, Indonesia.

Having gone through the contents of the book carefully, I feel confident that this book is quite simple and educative. The first three chapters take care of the initial introduction cum revision of the subject of dynamic positioning. These chapters are particularly beneficial for the learners who are new to the subject/. At the same time, these three chapters may easily be considered a good tool of revision of experienced DP professionals.

Chapters 4 to 15 are in the form of questions and answers, covering wide variety of topics important to the field of dynamic positioning. Questions and answers cover topics like environmental sensors, position reference sensors, thrusters, power management, DP operations, various tests & trials and documentations maintained onboard DP vessels.

I sincerely hope that Dr Kumar's efforts would be highly appreciated by the readers in the DP industry worldwide. The book has it all what it takes to be a good learning tool for the DP professionals on board and ashore. The book can be used as a reference material for dynamic positioning.

Happy reading!!

Mr Sugiman Layanto
Managing Director - PT Wintermar Offshore Marine Tbk
Chairman - INSA - Indonesian National Shipowners'
Association

PREFACE

When I look back, the first day I started the DP training preparations in 2007, a lot of developments took place in the field since then. Technology and versatility of simulators have been growing immensely. This has also influenced the learning and teaching process. One of the most enriching experience for me personally, has been the questions asked by the students. I have humbly realized that though the levels and types of questions asked on the subject of dynamic positioning in various countries I have taught DP, were different but one thing was common, each question asked by the students, made me learn this subject better. I take this opportunity to thank all my students who, by asking questions in my class, made it possible for me to write this book on questions and answers for dynamic positioning.

Questions asked in class, whether by a learner or by a teacher help and encourage the class to think aloud, facilitate learning and up to certain levels make the students confident. Encouraging students to ask questions also motivates then to learn better by being active participants in the learning process.

Questions in this book include very fundamental ones to understand the basic functioning of the DP system. At the same time, the book also includes the questions and their answers which address various aspects of Bloom's taxonomy of understanding, applying and evaluating the subject. I feel nothing works better than a question answered in a way that solves a problems of learning process. A student's understanding of the subject and levels of learning may be gauged by asking pertinent questions. On an average, in an educational environment, a teacher ends up asking about 300 questions a day. This may not so in case of maritime or DP training as simulators are being used and some questions may be self-answered by the students while exploring the simulators.

It is important for every DP professional to understand the system well that they are going operate or maintain. Keeping this in view, this book starts with an introduction to the functioning of DP system. Chapter two makes the reader aware of the six degrees of the movements. The understanding of the movements controlled by the DP system and the movements compensated for offsetting the readings of the position reference sensors is explained. Chapter three deals with the seven components of the DP system, how they connect with each other and how the controller controls the thruster output with the help of thruster allocation logic.

Chapter four to chapter fifteen contain the questions and answers. These chapters include questions and answers from basic functioning of the DP system, the sensor, position reference sensor, test on PRS, automation and networking used in DP system, various tests and trials conducted and importantly the operations related questions.

I take this opportunity to thank my teachers and students who taught me a lot. I thank my colleagues and team members at Sir Derek Bibby Maritime Training Centre, Global Maritime Training Centre, Aquamarine Maritime Academy, Mumbai, Ocean's XV DP Training centre, New Delhi, HIMT Offshore, Chennai, Maritronics DP Training Dubai, Korea Maritime and

Oceans University, Busan, Charkin DP Training center, Port Harcourt, Azureus Simulators Asia, Jakarta.

I also would like to thank my parents for their kind blessings, my wife Rajeshwari and my kids Rahul and Susmita, as without their contribution and perseverance, it would not have been possible to make this happen.

Dr Surender Kumar
(CEng, CMarEng, CMarTech, FIMarEST, FNI, fDPO, Ph.D)
Jakarta, 8th August 2020

SECTION – A: INTRODUCTION

CHAPTER 1
INTRODUCTION TO DYNAMIC POSITIONING

1.1 INTRODUCTION

Since its beginning in 1960's dynamic positioning very quickly moved from scientific research and geological surveys to offshore oil and gas industry. The safety of drilling operations at sea required a dependable automatic system so that the drill ship could be held in position during the operations. The credit for developing the dynamic positioning system goes to Howard Shatto.

1.2 BACKGROUND AND NEED OF DYNAMIC POSITIONING

The dynamic positioning is a maturing technology, having its origin in the United States of America. It was the innovative ideas of Howard Shatto (Jr) that led to the achievement of the world's first automatic control of vessel to hold its position while carrying out drilling operations. (Continental, Union, Shell and Superior Oil) normally known as CUSS 1. This was the first ship controlled by thrusters and positioned for drilling applications.

Initially, the Cuss 1 was a marine barge, which was modified and rebuilt into a deep-water drilling vessel. Howard Shatto, who was instrumental in building Shell's and the world's first thruster controlled and diesel electric drilling rig, is also remembered as the person who led a team in the development of The world's first dynamic positioning vessel with automatic control. It was Shatto's ideas that the world's first automatic control by DP, worked for the company's drill ship known as Eureka core drillship in 1960. Electronic controllers were used from Honeywell to control the three movements of the vessel namely surge, sway and yaw. Howard Shatto and his team continued to work for the safety of drilling operations and made the first DP rig which used a riser system and blow out preventer (BOP) for oil well drilling. This DP rig was the iconic SEDCO 445 built for Shell in 1971.

1.3 DEVELOPMENT OF DP SYSTEM

The development of the dynamic positioning can be easily understood by the block diagram as depicted below.

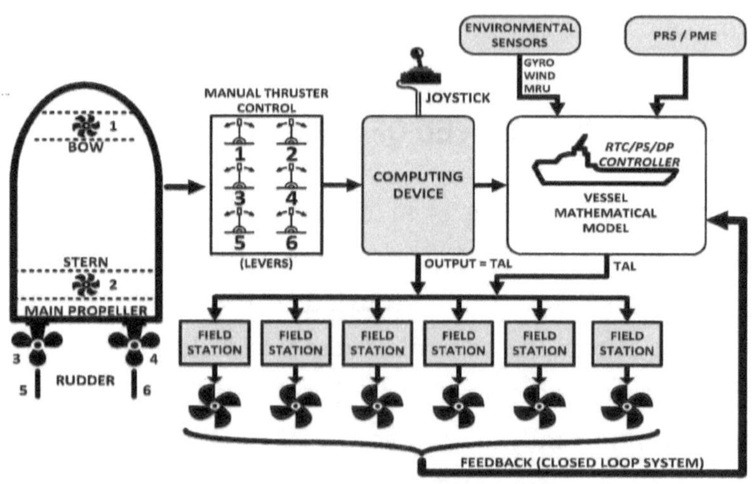

Fig. 1.1 Development of DP System

The control of main propulsion system and thrusters was being done from the engine room as directed and decided by the bridge to begin with. This had its own drawbacks and communication problems were adding more to the difficulties. This was followed by the upgradation of the controls and bringing the controls to the bridge. This made it easy for the bridge watch keepers to control the thrusters and propulsion as required.

The control of thrusters from bridge had a challenge as the number of thrusters had to be controlled by an individual control lever. This was quickly followed by a single lever called Joystick controlling the ship movements. The input from joystick was processed based on movement/s and direction. Basis this an output was created by the computer attached with the joystick. This output is known as the thruster allocation logic (TAL). The advancements in the field of computers brought in more capable and faster computers. The computers used with joysticks were also replaced with faster computers and were called real time computers (RTC) as they had the capabilities oy process the input on real time basis, and thereafter generating output to control thruster output (TAL).

The RTC was given inputs from the environmental sensors (Gyro, wind sensor and motion reference unit (MRU) and the position reference sensors (PRS). There was an arrangement made to feed the mathematical model to this computer. By now, with these all inputs, this RTC has become a very capable and loaded with lots of information. This was processed and an output in the form of TAL was generated to control the thrusters automatically and getting a feedback from the thrusters under the control of RTC. It is interesting to note here that everything is an input to the RTC except the TAL. The thrust allocation logic is the only output from the RTC. This output has got four components namely,

- How much thrust?

- To which all thrusters?

- Which direction?

- How much time?

Once the allocated thrusters have developed the required amount of thrust to keep the vessel in position, a feedback is sent to the RTC.

1.4 USE OF DYNAMIC POSITIONING

Though the development of the dynamic positioning technology was started keeping in view the safety aspects for drilling operations, yet it took the whole offshore industry applications in its fold.

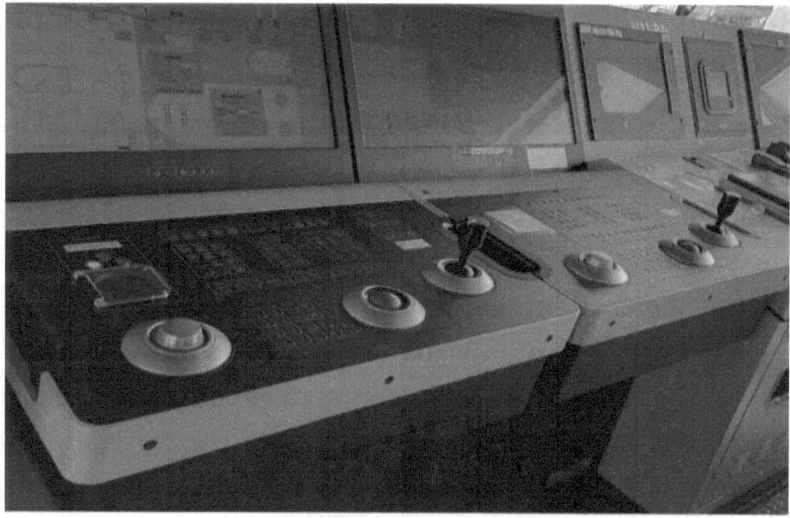

Fig: 1.2 DP System Installed onboard (Courtesy Kongsberg and Wintermar)

As the technology provided safety never before available, it soon became popular and was applied to other types of vessel in the offshore oil and gas industry. Currently the dynamic positioning is being used on the following types of ships worldwide (but not limited to).

- Drilling

- Diving support

- ROV support

- Cable Layers

- Pipe Layers

- Supply vessels

- Well Stimulation

- Dredgers

- Rock Dumping

- Anchor handling

- Shuttle tankers

- Floating Production Storages and Offloading (FPSO)

- Wind Service (with Jack up)

1.5 CONCLUSION

Dynamic positioning as a system and as a technology is here to stay and grow stronger as it is finding new areas and applications. The humble beginning from the drilling ships, spreading over to all the safety critical areas of the offshore oil and gas sector speaks for itself. The earlier guidelines IMO/MSC/645 continue to be in force for the vessel built before the new guidelines IMO/MSC/1580 came in to effect from June 2017 onwards.

CHAPTER 2
THE SIX DEGREES OF MOVEMENT/ FREEDOM

2.1 INTRODUCTION

Any freely floating structure including a ship will be affected by the forces acting on to it. The forces may be due to wind, wave and current. The amount of the force and direction will impact and thus results into a movement of the ship. The movements can be divided into two axis, horizontal and vertical.

2.2 MOVEMENTS ON HORIZONTAL PLANE

2.2.1 SURGE

Surge is the movement on the horizontal plane caused by the environmental forces acting on the vessel. This movement will result into forward and aft motion of the ship.

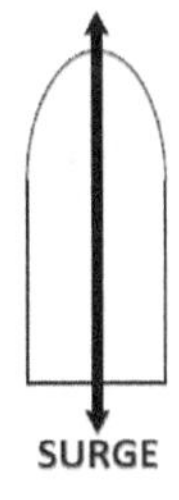

Fig. 2.1 Surge

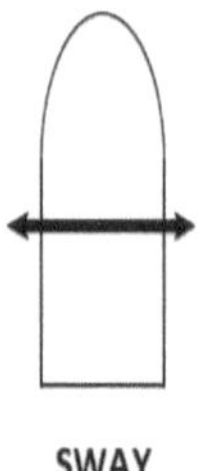

Fig. 2.2   Sway

2.2.2 SWAY

This movement on the horizontal plane causes the ship to move athwartship to port or to starboard. The environmental forces acting on the windage area or area below water where current and waves have effects, will cause the ships movement.

Both the movements, the surge and the sway as discussed above are measured by position reference sensor (PRS) or position measuring equipment (PME).

2.2.3 YAW

The third movement around the horizontal axis, the yaw, is measured by gyro, which is an environmental sensor. The gyro gives important input about the ships rotation around the centre of rotation (COR), the heading, as selected by the DP operator. The gyro also gives the rate of turn (ROT).

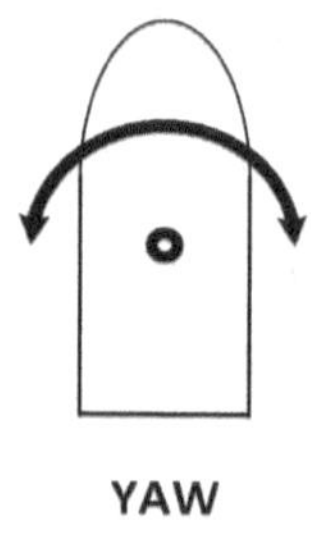

Fig. 2.3   Yaw

2.3 MOVEMENTS ON VERTICAL PLANE

2.3.1 ROLL

Roll movement of the vessel is around the vertical axis to the port or to the starboard. The vessel may roll without losing her position. This side to side tilting movement of the ship, through the centre of the ship. Roll movement may cause the offsetting of the position reference sensors, thereby sending wrong position to the DP controller. The earliest ships were making use of inclinometers to measure this movement along with the pitch. Two separate inclinometers were used for the purpose.

2.3.2 PITCH

Pitching is the movement of the vessel around the vertical axis which makes the ship move (tilt) forward and aft. Pitching also offsets the position reference sensors and giving wrong signals.

Both, the roll and the pitch movements of the vessel are measured and offset/compensated for the movements of the vessel's position reference sensors. The offsetting or compensation helps in not resulting in unnecessary movements using power and thrusters and helps in better position keeping of the vessel.

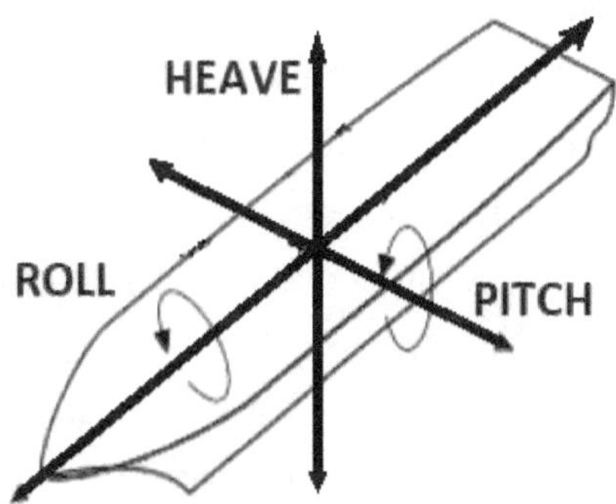

Fig. 2.4 Roll, Pitch and Heave Movements

2.3.3 HEAVE

All the movements mentioned above, the roll, the pitch and the heave are measured by vertical reference unit (VRU) or vertical reference sensor (VRS) or motion reference unit (MRU). VRU/VRS are can measure roll and pitch movements, whereas the MRU can measure all three movements. Most modern DP vessels are now fitted with MRU's. measuring heave becomes very important for certain applications such as diving, drilling, accommodations barges in particular. The diving bell stabilization is considered very important for safe operations.

These movements may have adverse effects on the ship's movements, human and machinery performances. The design of most DP vessels is in such way that the hull shape helps in keeping the roll and pitch motions under control.

2.4 CONCLUSION

It is important to understand the six degrees of freedom of a vessel. The three degrees which are measured and controlled using active thrust with the help of mathematical model and the DP controller or the process station. Also, the other three degrees of freedom on the vertical plane, which are not controlled, but two of them i.e. roll and pitch are compensated for the movement of the position reference sensors. So, measuring the roll and pitch also becomes very important from that perspective. Surge and sway are measured by the PRS. Yaw is measured by gyro. The roll and pitch movements of the vessel, which need to be compensated for are measured by VRU/VRS/MRU.

CHAPTER 3
THE SEVEN COMPONENTS OF DYNAMIC POSITIONING

3.1 INTRODUCTION

Dynamic positioning is an art and science to keeping vessel in a particular position or moving in a particular direction at particular speed and a particular rate of turn, with the help of the thrust generated by its own thrusters. This thrust is often referred to as "Active thrust:"

According to IMO/MSC 645, a dynamically positioned vessel (DP-vessel) may be defined as means a unit or a vessel/ship, which is capable of maintaining its position automatically. The position includes fixed location or predetermined track, moving at a speed/rate of turn for heading. These movements are controlled exclusively by means of thruster force, which is generated by the ship's own thrusters.

According to IMO/MSC 1580, a dynamically positioned vessel (DP vessel) may be defined as a ship or a unit or a vessel, which can maintain its position including heading automatically. The vessels position or heading may be fixed or may be moving relative location or predetermined track, following a set pattern of speed or heading change. This is achieved by means of thruster force generated by the ship's own thrusters. More often this thrust is referred to as the active thrust.

3.2 SUB-SYSTEMS OF DYNAMIC POSITIONING (DP)

According to IMO/MSC 645 and IMO/MSC/1580 the dynamic positioning system has been divided in to three sub systems as below.

1. DP Controls

2. Power System

3. Thruster system

Power System is consisting of the prime movers including their auxiliaries and pipelines, alternators, power management system, distribution system including cables and cable routing. The thruster system consists of all what it takes to supply the required thrust for the vessel to hold position. The thrusters are controlled by the output of the DP controller generally known as the thrust allocation logic (TAL). The DP control essentially includes all the subsystem needed for controlling the functioning of the system. This includes the DP controller, environmental sensors, position reference sensors, hardware commonly referred to as HMI, including displays and the operator.

3.3 THE SEVEN COMPONENTS

The DP system is divided into seven components. When all components work together well, the DP system functions as one system. The seven components for ease of understanding are power, thruster, environmental sensors, position reference sensors, DP controller, hardware generally referred to as HMI and the operator.

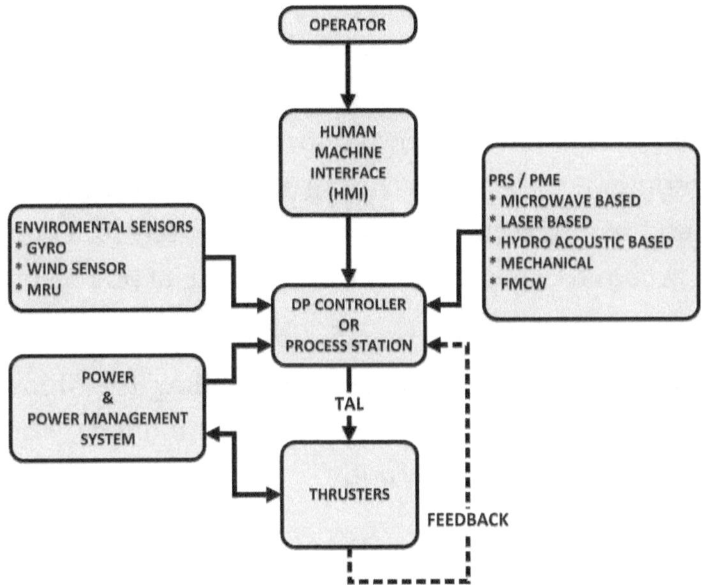

Fig: 3.1   DP System/Sub-system/Components

3.3.1 POWER

Depending upon the class of the vessel the power system installed onboard may have the required levels of redundancy. The power system consists of the prime mover, usually diesel engine, alternator, cables, switchboard, bus tie breakers and power management system. For DP class 1 and a DP class 2 vessel, the cables may not be arranged separately/different routes but for a DP class 3 vessel, it is mandatory to ensure proper redundancy by having a set of cables laid into a separated route protected by A/60 bulkhead. The same is applicable for the switchboards for a DP 3 vessel.

The power system for DP enabled vessels is expected to have a suitable response time to power demand changes during operations. For a DP class 1vessel, the power system onboard, may not be redundant and no back up provided. For DP class 2 vessels the power plant and system is recommended to be divided into minimum two parts so that in case one power system fails, the other system, which is isolated safely, from the first one, will be able to provide power for the operations to be safely terminated thereby assuring safety. Depending upon the design and requirements, the power system may function as one system or may be split into two with the help of bus tie breakers.

DP classes 2 and 3 are required to have power management system (PMS) which is capable of controlling the ships power automatically. This must meet the redundancy and class requirements to avoid black out.

3.3.2 THRUSTERS

As per 1.2.23 of the IMO/MSC/1580, ships thruster system may include all components and systems and sub systems which are considered necessary to make sure it can supply the vessel's dynamic positioning system the necessary thrust force required for keeping the ship in position or making a move at a required speed and rate of turn. Generally, a thruster system may include the following.

- Thrusters drive units with the required auxiliary systems including the pipelines associated.

- Hydraulic system, cooling and lubricating needed for the complete system.

- The main propeller systems and the main rudders of the vessel are also considered part of the ships thruster system if the same are controlled by the DP system.

- Thruster control system or thruster control electronics or field stations

- Manual thruster controls for each thruster

- Associated cables and routing of the cable especially for the DP class 3 vessels.

Modern-day DP vessels may be fitted with several thrusters and varying types of thrusters depending upon the equipment class, design criteria and type of jobs the vessel may be engaged in. Bow and stern thrusters are usually required to turn the vessel for controlling yaw movements along with the sway moments of the vessel. These thrusters are also called as tunnel thrusters as they are fitted inside a tunnel.

Some vessels may have arrangements that azimuth thrusters will provide the main propulsion, whereas other vessel may have a conventional main propellers and main rudders for this purpose, but under the control of DP system. All propulsion devices under the control of DP systems are referred to as thrusters. Some special vessels may have special types of thrusters such as Voith Schneider Propellers (VSP), retractable thrusters and some other special applications thruster devices.

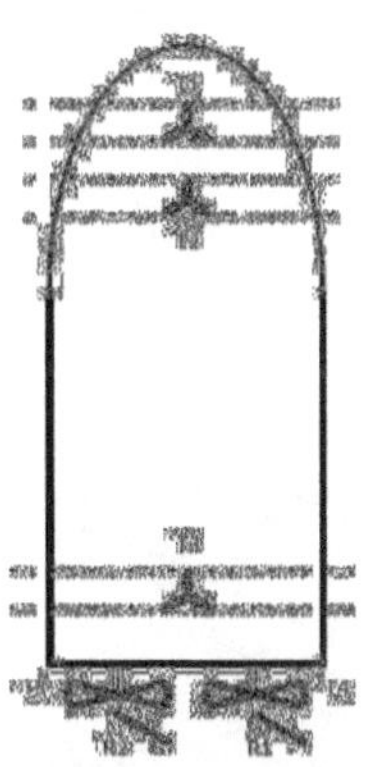

Fig: 3.2   Thrusters

All types of thruster are controlled by the DP controllers with the help of signals. The output signal or the command signals is sent from DP controller to respective thruster and once the command is activated by the thrusters, a feedback signal is sent by the thrusters to the DP controller. Comparing the command and feedback signal is considered an important method to see if the thrusters are functioning well.

3.3.3 ENVIRONMENTAL SENSORS

DP vessels are acted upon by the environmental forces. These forces make the vessel move. Some of these movements are making the vessels move forward and aft and port and starboard of the ship. These movements are measured by the position reference sensors. The other movement may cause the vessel to change her heading. This movement and rate of turn are measured by the gyro compass. The three commonly used environmental sensors are as below.

- Wind Sensor

- Motion reference Sensor

- Gyro

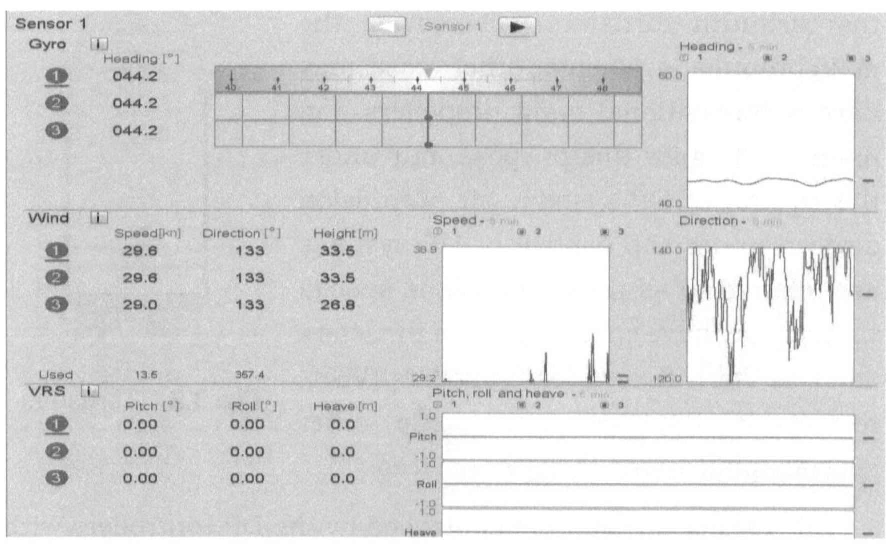

Fig: 3.3   Environmental Sensors (Courtesy Kongsberg)

The wind sensor measures the speed of the wind and its direction. As the wind acts upon the windage area/sale area of the ship and that may result into some movement (drifting). To avoid this unwanted movement, the DP system must generate an equal and opposite thrust force. This is possible only if the force of the wind, which is called wind force vector is accurately measured. Wind sensor measures the speed of the wind acting on the vessel and also measures the rate of turn.

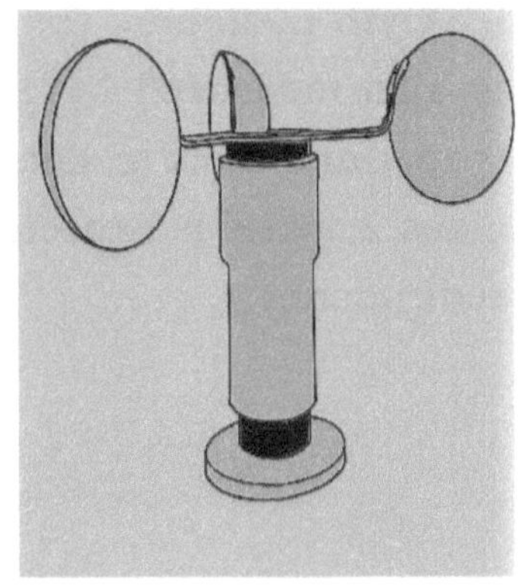

Fig: 3.4 Wind Sensor

Due to wind and other force's effects on the vessel, the vessel may start rolling, pitching or heaving. These movements are taking place around the vertical axis. Roll and pitch movements may cause unwanted movements of the position reference sensors. If the vessel must keep the position, the unwanted movements of the position reference sensors must be compensated for. So, these movements are measured and given to the DP controller and are compensated for. Vertical reference Unit (VRU) or Vertical reference Sensors (VRS) are designed to measure roll and pitch movements of the vessel. Motion reference Unit (MRU) can measure all three movements i.e. roll, pitch and heave. Most modern DP vessels are installed with MRUs.

Fig: 3.5 Motion Reference Unit (MRU) (Courtesy Kongsberg)

Gyro measures the heading of the vessel. The rate of turn is also measured by gyro. Depending the class of the vessel, gyro numbers are decided to be installed on a vessel. A DP class 2 vessel is expected to have three gyros for the purpose of redundancy.

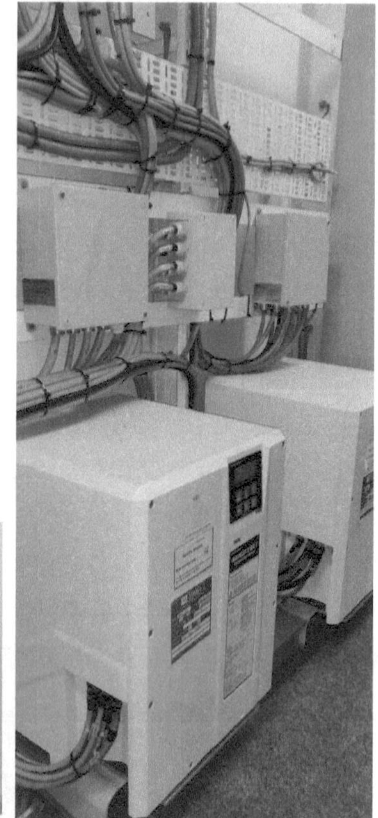
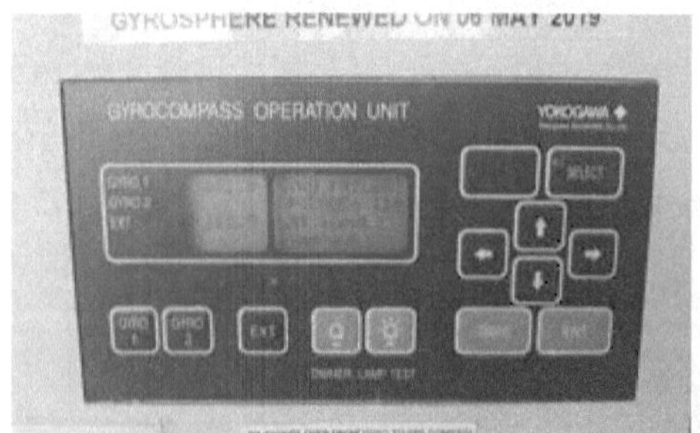

Fig: 3.6   Gyro Compass

3.3.4 POSITION REFERENCE SENSORS

Position reference sensors (PRS) or Position Measuring Equipment (PME) as they are commonly known as are the sensors which measure the ships position. The position here means the movement of the ship for the surge and the sway of the vessel on the horizontal plane. To know and control the surge and sway movements these must be measured. So, at least one PRS is must to put the vessel on DP mode to control the surge and sway movements automatically. A DP class 1 vessel needs to have at least two PRS active. Both the PRS on a DP class 1 vessel must not be of the same type. It simply means that they must be working on two different principles. For a DP class 2 and class 3 vessel the minimum number of PRS is three. When two or more PRS are installed, it is recommended that they are not all the same type (working on the same principle). This is to avoid the common modes of failure of the PRS. Due consideration must be given to the fact that the PRS are suitable for the type of operating conditions of the vessel. The following are the principles of operation for the PRS used onboard DP vessels.

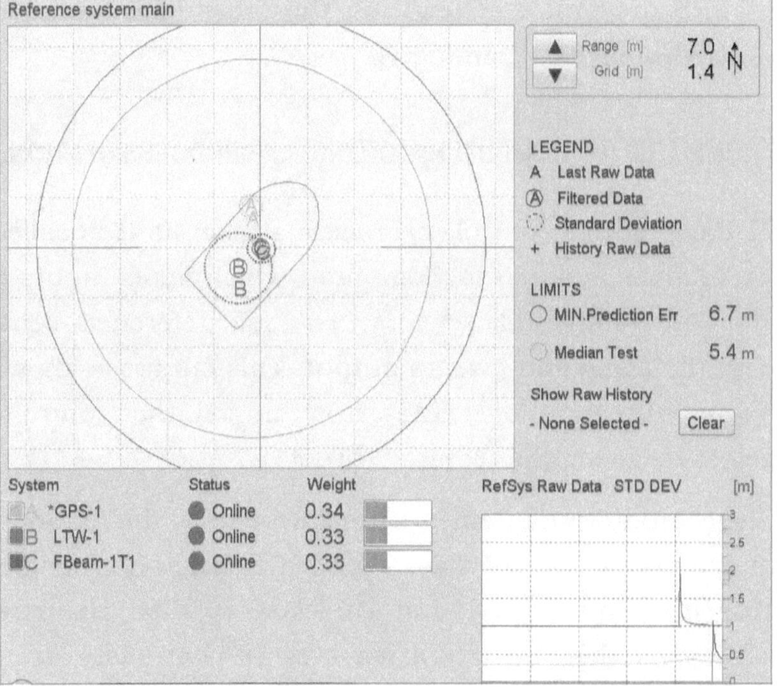

Fig: 3.7   Position Reference Sensors (Courtesy Kongsberg)

1. Radar (Microwave): The PRS working on this principle are the Artemis and the DGPS.

2. LASER Radars: The laser radars based PRS are Fanbeam, Cyscan and Spot Track.

3. Hydro- Acoustics: The two commonly used acoustics based PRS are HPR and Hipap.

4. Mechanical: The mechanical movement of the sensor is made by the wire used in a Tautwire system. This PRS is considered the most dependable PRS as it doesn't have a signal disturbance due to noise.

5. Frequency Modulated continuous radars (FMCW radars): The Radius and Radascan are the two new generation radars being used for position keeping of the DP vessels. Being based on a new technology, the efficiency of these PRS are much better than the other PRS under given environmental conditions.

3.3.5 COMPUTER (DP COMPUTER)/CONTROLLER/PROCESS STATION

The DP computer/Controller/Process station as it is called by various names is a special computer, which takes inputs from various environmental sensors, position reference sensors, process the same and give an output. This output is known as the thrust allocation logic (TAL). It is this TAL that controls the thrusters by giving the required thrust.

The computer requirements are governed by the redundancy requirements of the DP class. For a DP class 1, a single DP controller is sufficient. For a DP class 2, dual redundancy mandates that there must be at least two DP controllers installed. For a DP class 3 the requirement is to have three controllers, one of these controllers must be installed in A/60 bulkhead separated compartment to meet the redundancy requirements.

Fig: 3.8   DP Controller – (Courtesy Kongsberg)

It is good practice and a requirement that the DP computers are isolated from other on-board computing devices and communication devices thereby ensuring various interfaces with the DP system such as command and feedback work smoothly. DP system integrity is ensured by the connection of various computers/computing devices used the DP system using networking.

Fig: 3.9 DP Controller – (Courtesy Converteam)

Usually a standard set of hardware and software is made use of to achieve this and tested at regular intervals to ensure prevention of unauthorized/unwanted devices or systems to be connected to the DP computers/system.

3.3.6 THE HARDWARE/HMI

All the hardware which a DP operator may use to control the DP system are called the human machine interface (HMI). HMI must be designed operations centric so that it makes the job of the operator easy and ergonomically safe.

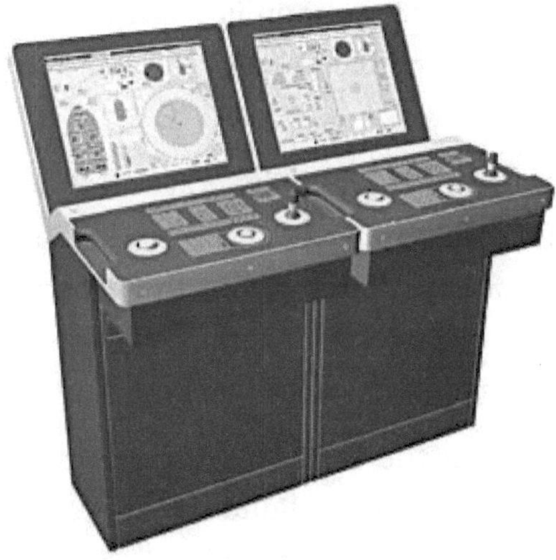

Fig: 3.10   Human Machine Interface (HMI) (Courtesy Kongsberg)

All HMI including the display systems and the DP control station are designed to suit the ergonomic principles that ensures proper operation of the DP system with ease. The manual joystick, or manual control of thrusters using individual control levers are also included in the hardware. Entering of the required data for operations, adjusting brightness, accessing menu and submenu, various push buttons for activating/deactivating sensors/PRS/ modes etc are important part of HMI. HMI redundancy is also decided by the class requirements. Various views and dialogue boxes help the DP operator to feed in the required data and set the various sensors and other machinery as required for the operations.

3.3.7 THE OPERATOR

Dynamic positioning operators (DPOs) are appropriately qualified and experienced personnel who operate the DP system. Usually they are the deck watchkeeping officers who have graduated to be a DPOs after following a recognized scheme of training.

Nautical Institute (NI) London is a once such internationally recognized body responsible for the training and certification of DP operato4rs.

The NI promulgates the qualification and training schemes for the DPOs. The training must be completed followed by requisite number of days of experience before the prospective DPOs can submit their documents for verification and acceptance by the NI. Once the NI is satisfied, the candidate gets his/her DP certificate.

The first phase of the DPO training starts with attending a DP Induction course. The candidate on successfully completing this phase is issued with a certificate of completion and a logbook. The logbook must be completed for the required tasks/ experience whist onboard a DP enabled vessel.in the second phase. On completion of the second phase the candidate returns to the training centre for an advanced DP training called DP simulator course. This phase gets completed if the student undertakes the courses successfully by appearing and passing an online test. During the next phase the prospective DPO logs in the required number of days in DP logbook issued earlier and completes the required tasks. On completion of this the senior DPO and the Master recommends the candidate suitable for the job of a DPO. On completion of these all steps, the candidate sends the completed records to the NI for verification. If all found meeting the requirements, the candidate is then issued with a DPO certificate, which may be limited or unlimited depending on the types of vessel and DP system worked on.

3.4 CONCLUSION

The chapter starts with an introduction about the seven components of the dynamic positioning system. Thereafter it introduces the readers to the required details of each component crisply. Every DP professional would be keen to understand the seven components well before exploring the DP system further.

SECTION – B: QUESTIONS AND ANSWERS

CHAPTER 4

BASICS OF DYNAMIC POSITIONING & SIX DEGREES OF FREEDOM

1. What is dynamic positioning?

    Dynamic positioning is an art and science to keeping vessel in a particular position or moving in a particular direction at particular speed and a particular rate of turn, with the help of the thrust generated by its own thrusters. This thrust is often referred to as "Active thrust:"

    According to IMO/MSC 645, a dynamically positioned vessel (DP-vessel) may be defined as means a unit or a vessel/ship, which is capable of maintaining its position automatically. The position includes fixed location or predetermined track, moving at a speed/rate of turn for heading.

    According to IMO/MSC 1580, a dynamically positioned vessel (DP vessel) may be defined as a ship or a unit or a vessel, which can maintain its position including heading automatically. This is achieved by means of thruster force generated by the ship's own thrusters. More often this thrust is referred to as the active thrust.

2.   What are the Seven Components of DP System?

A system is usually consisted of sub systems and sub systems are consisted of components. The DP system is divided into sub systems, namely DP control system, Thruster system and power system. The below given components make the DP system.

- Power

- Thrusters

- Environmental Sensors

- Position Reference Sensors (PRS/PME)

- Computer (RTC/DPC/Controller)

- MMI/HMI

- Operator

3.   Name the Six Degrees of Freedom or Six Degrees of Movements?

A free-floating vessel or a structure at sea will have certain forces acting upon it. The major among them is the wind force. Which is measured by wind sensors. The other forces are current and certain work-related forces. Due to effect of these forces on the vessel, there are some resultant movements. These movements are divided into two. One the movements of the horizontal plane and two the movements on the vertical plane.

The movements of the horizontal plane are known as surge, sway and yaw. The movements on the vertical plane are known as roll, pitch and heave.

4.   Which movements of the vessel are controlled?

The movement on the horizontal plane are measured and controlled. These are surge, sway and yaw. The yaw is measured by gyro and controlled by using thrusters. The surge and the sway are measured by the position reference sensors or position measuring equipment and controlled by using thrusters.

5. Which movements of the vessel are not controlled?

Vessel's movement on the vertical plane are not controlled. It means that these movements on the vertical plane, namely the pitch, roll and heave movements are not controlled. These movements are being measured by motion reference unit (MRU). It is interesting to note here that though these motions are being measured but never controlled. Two movements i.e. roll and pitch are compensated for the movements of PRS.

6. If the pitch, roll and heave movements are not controlled, why are these measured?

Pitch roll and heave movements of the ship are measured but not controlled. The pitch and roll movements are affecting the location of the position reference sensors. These movements are measured and fed to the DP controller to offset/compensate the roll and pitch movements for the reference sensors. This can avoid unnecessary use of thrusters and thus save power.

7. What does 'Upstream' mean in the offshore industry?

Upstream relates to the activities of exploration, extraction and production of oil and gas.

8. What does 'Downstream' mean in the offshore industry?

After the oil is handed over ashore for the processing the "Downstream" starts. The downstream activities include refining of crude oil and thereafter the processing and purifying. The marketing and distribution of various petroleum products are also included in this segment.

9.   What does 'Midstream' mean in the offshore industry?

One of the important steps in oil and gas industry to refine the product received from the drilling sites. This activity is called the midstream. Midstream may also include activities like storage, transportation, marketing and production of tertiary products. More often these days the midstream and downstream are merged together due to a thin boundary between the various activities.

10.   What was the reason to develop a Dynamic Positioning system?

In deep water it is not possible to use jack-up rigs. It was not safe to use anchored vessels for drilling. So, for the safe drilling operations, the DP system was invented.

11.   What is the prime function of the DP?

The prime function of dynamic positioning system is to ensure that the ship should maintain her position (surge and sway) and heading (yaw), with the help of active thrust. Active thrust is generated by the ship's own thrusters. Based on the sensors input the amount of thrust is decided by the DP controller.

12.   Which all movements of the ship do the DP System control?

The three movements of the ship on horizontal plane are first measured by the sensors and controlled by the DP system. These are yaw, sway and surge. The two moments i.e. sway and surge are measured by various position reference sensors. The third movement i.e. yaw is measured by the gyro. These measurements become the basis of the chain further to control the movements by using active thrust.

13. Does the DP System control the ship's pitching motion?

    No, the pitching is not controlled by the DP system. Roll and pitch motion of the ship are measured by vertical reference unit (VRU) or vertical reference sensor (VRS). If the vessel is fitted with a motion reference unit (MRU), then all three movements on the vertical plane can be measured. The two movements namely roll and pitch are measure and compensated for the movement of the position reference sensors.

14. If the DP system loses all reference systems after it has been on DP for several hours. What will happen to the ship?

    The ship be able to maintain her position for some time, till there is big change in weather conditions. This is possible due to the "Model Control" or "Dead Reckoning". After the sensors have been lost, the mathematical model will remember the last known position and try to maintain the vessels position.

15. What is the value "Current", DP Current" or the "Current as Residual" as indicated on the DP position plot page?

    The value indicated as the Current/DP current/Residual as Current are indicated as the sum total of unmeasured forces acting on the vessel. The vessel faces two types of the forces. One is measured and other one is not measured. The measured one if the wind force. Which is measured by the wind sensors. The remaining forces are calculated by the computer and indicated as the" Current", DP Current" or "Residual as Current ". This displayed on the position plotting view of the DP system.

Fig: 4.1 Residual as Current or DP Current (Courtesy Kongsberg)

16. What is the meaning of redundancy with respect to DP systems?

The literal meaning of redundancy is being in the state of no longer needed or no longer being useful. This implies that the once something is redundant, do we have something else to do the same function. This calls for understanding redundancy in the concept that there must be a backup. As per the IMO MSC/645 the redundancy may be defined as ability of a component or system of dynamic positioning to help maintain or restore its function after a single failure has taken place.

17. How can we achieve redundancy?

There are different ways redundancy can be achieved. One such method is installation of multiple components/ subsystems or systems. This simply applies that adding more equipment and thereby creating back up. Redundancy can also be created by providing some alternative means of performing the function, which the failed equipment was performing.

18. What are sub-systems of Dynamic Positioning System as per IMO MSC 645?

As per IMO/MSC/645, the DP system is divided in to three subsystems, i.e. DP-controls, thruster system and power system. The DP control includes the hardware (HMI), environmental sensors, position reference sensors, the DP computer (Controller) and the operator. That makes the complete seven components of the DP system.

19. **What is 'FSVAD'?**

It stands for Flag State Verification Acceptance Document. FSVAD is issued by the classification society after carrying out DP trials. The flag state administration issues this document on an approved format to a ship which complies with the prescribed guidelines.

20. **What is DPVAD?**

It stands for Dynamic Positioning Verification Acceptance Document (DPVAD). As per the new guidelines from the IMO (IMO/MSC 1580), DPVAD is to be issued, once the vessel completes prescribed survey and testing as per the guidance available in the said document.

21. **What does "position keeping" mean according IMO MSC 645?**

Position keeping doesn't necessarily mean a fixed position. The vessel may move but within defined limits. The purpose of position keeping is to keep the vessel's position with in the normal excursion limits These excursion limits are defined by the DP control system used and prevalent environmental conditions.

22. **What is minimum number of DP controllers/Process Stations required for DP class 1 vessel??**

DP class 1 or equipment class 1 is designed to have single redundancy or literally no back up. Hence one controller is enough for the DP class 1 DP systems.

23. What is minimum number of DP controllers/Process Stations required for DP class 2 vessel??

    DP class 2 or equipment class 2vessels are designed to have dual redundancy. Hence keeping in view, the backup requirements, the DP class 2 vessels are expected to have two controllers.

24. What is minimum number of DP controllers/Process Stations required for DP class 3 vessel??

    DP 3 vessels are designed to have triple redundancy. One of the redundancies back must be provided in a separate compartment isolated by A/60 bulkhead. Hence DP 3 vessels must be fitted with three controllers. Two of the controllers may be installed in one compartment and third controller must be installed in an "A/60" separated compartment.

25. What are the basic requirements of IMO Class 3/equipment class 3/DP Class 3 installation?

    DP control system of a DP class 3 vessel may comprise of a duplex or triplex system fitted in one compartment. This to be backed up by yet another system in an A60 separated compartment.

26. A vessel has a Classification Society notation of DP(AA). What does this mean?

    This notation indicates that Complies with the Equipment Class requirements for Class 2. This notation is used by LR class. Similarly there other equivalent notations for DP class 2 by other class societies.

27. How many position reference sensors may be required as a minimum for DP Class 2 Operations?

    A DP class 2 operation requires minimum three PRS. All three PRS must not be working on the same principle of operation. Of course, two of them may be based on the same principles of operation. This arrangement is made to ensure that a failure based on common mode or common fault is avoided. This also ensures total loss of PRS.

28. What is the main function of redundancy in DP system?

Redundancy in a DP system allows the operation to be safely abandoned after any single-point failure occurs. The redundancy provided will help the vessel to maintain her position and heading till operations are safely abandoned.

29. How catastrophic failures within a DP system are avoided?

The provision of redundancy helps in ensuring safe termination of work and hence the catastrophic failures may be avoided because there is redundancy.

30. What is a vessel model?

The vessel model which may at times be also referred to as mathematical model, is a mathematical description of how the vessel reacts to the forces acting upon it. For this purpose, the vessel is divided into two parts i.e. aerodynamic characteristics and the hydrodynamic characteristics of the vessel.

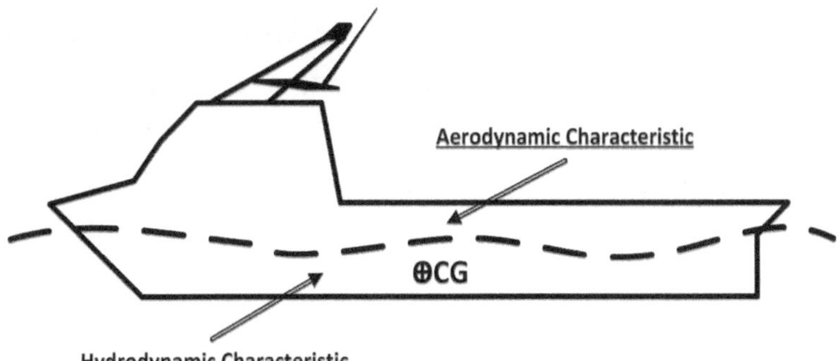

Fig: 4.2   Vessel Mathematical Model

Vessels aerodynamic and hydro dynamic characteristics make the mathematical model which decides how the vessel reacts to the environmental forces acting on the vessel.

31. A DP system is divided into seven components. Which component is used by the DP operator to receive and send various information/data? This component also has various input controls. Which component are we discussing about?

    The DPO uses the human machine interface (HMI) which combinations of all the hardware used in DP station. The HMI is used to communicate with the DP controller, activate and setting up of various sensors and thrusters.

32. Which one degree/s of freedom/movement is/are monitored, but NOT controlled, by the DP system?

    The DP system measures the roll and pitch movements by using VRU (or MRU for measuring heave) but does not control these. The measurement is for the purpose of compensating or offsetting the movements of the position reference sensors.

33. The value of Current/DP Current/Residual as Current as shown on the DP screen may be inaccurate. What is reason for this?

    The value shown on the DP screen which may be shown as Current/DP Current/Residual as Current. This not the sea current, this value indicates the total sum of unknown forces. This is not measured but calculated by the DP computer.

34. Wind force acting on the vessel is measured by wind sensor. Which other forces are acting on the ship and how are they measured?

    All other forces other the wind, are called the residual force. These are not measured but calculated. This is displayed on the DP page as Current/DP current/Residual as current.

35. There is need to consider lots of data to be taken into the DP mathematical model. This data may be a combination of calculated and real time forces. Which real time force are used in mathematical model?

    The only real time data (measured) comes from the wind sensor. The wind speed and direction are measured and fed into the mathematical model.

36. What movement of the vessel requires heading control?

    The yaw movement of the vessels results in the change of heading of the vessel. The gyro picks up the heading change, applies to the controller, which in turn will allocate some thruster/s to correct the heading.

37. What does the wind direction and strength in relation to the ship's head do to the mathematical model?

    Some of the important data taken into the mathematical model is dependent upon the form of the vessel above the waterline, i.e. the "sail area" or the "aerodynamic characteristics) and its disposition. This area is affected by the wind speed and direction and hence the mathematical model is affected in turn.

CHAPTER 5
DIFFERENT TYPES OF DP VESSELS AND THEIR APPLICATIONS

1. For a pipe laying DP vessel, in addition to the normal PRS and environmental sensors, what other special sensors may be used and why?

    In addition to PRS and environmental sensors a pipe laying vessel will need input from the stinger sensors. This gives an important input of the additional forces due to pipe acting on the vessel. The vessel DP system must know and compensate these additional forces.

2. A DP vessel is fitted with 2 tunnels thrusters forward, 2 tunnel thrusters aft, 2 main engines/propellers/rudders. Main propellers are pitch control type. During DP operations the Port main propeller fails to full ahead pitch causing a drive off towards nearby platform. What should the DPOs do?

    The first and the most important thing to be done by the DPO, is to identify the failed thruster/propeller and activate emergency stop for the failed thruster at the earliest.

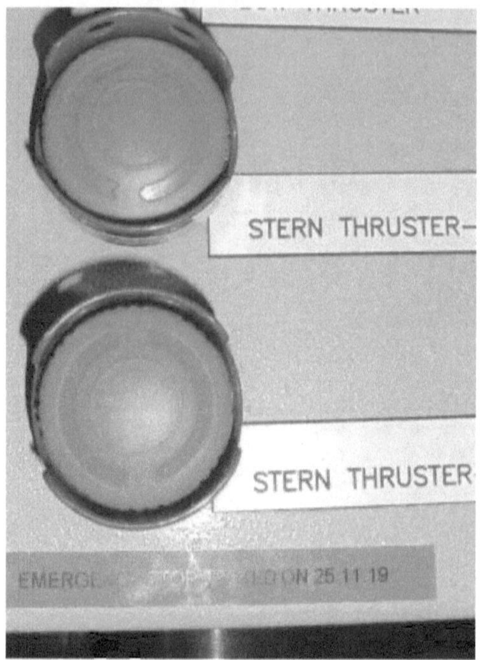

Fig: 5.1 Emergency Stop Switch

3. Which type of vessel used the first DP system?

The first DP vessel was a drill ship. DP was invented for the safety of drilling operations. Though later it became very popular and now dynamic positioning is being used in variety of operations in the offshore and marine industry.

4. What is the role of a remotely operated vehicle (ROV) support vessel?

ROV support vessel assists the ROV to be safely launched, operated and recovered. This vessel may have added redundancy for the purpose. Depending upon the type of ROV onboard, ROV support vessel may have launching and recovery system accordingly. To follow the ROV during the operations ROV vessel uses a DP mode called follow target or follow sub mode of DP operation.

Fig: 5.2   (a) ROV with Launching arrangements and Umbilical (b) ROV Support Vessel

5.   What is a cable laying vessel?

A cable layer or cable laying vessel is used to lay cable or repair cables already laid. These vessels have capability to work in shallow to deep waters and are designed accordingly. While laying/repairing cable, the vessel may use track follow or auto track mode as may be applicable. The cable carousel onboard may have capacity of storing cable of thousands of tons. Also new cable laying vessels may have capabilities to lay cable in ice waters.

6.   What is role of diving support vessel?

Various activities in offshore may require continuous intervention at the subsea level for smooth production of oil and gas. Subsea intervention may require divers to be launched and recovered. The DSVs are used for this purpose. Safe launch/recovery of divers, whether in open waters or close to an asset is a very risky affair, so must be done safely.

7.   What is the main function of pipelay vessel?

The main purpose of a pipe lay vessel is to assist in seabed pipe laying and pipe repairing activities. Along with maintaining position it is also important for a pipe laying vessel to maintain the tension on pipe.

8. **What are the other activities onboard a pipe laying vessel?**

   For accomplishing pipe laying operations, a pipe layer may utilize services like ROV, crane, subsea crane, survey and inspection activities simultaneously.

9. **What is recommended class of a pipe lay vessel?**

   Though there are no rules applicable here but as per IMCA guidelines and recommendations a DP 2 or DP 3 would be preferred for the pipe laying activities. Better redundancy will help to maintain the pipeline integrity.

10. **What is heavy lift or crane vessel?**

    A heavy lift or crane vessel is used in offshore industrial missions where heavy loads need to be picked up/placed. These vessels may be mono hull or may be semi sub type. The design will depend upon the applications and the areas of operation. Most large lift vessel usually work till surface level or very shallow depths.

11. **What precautions must be taken while operating a heavy lift/crane vessel?**

    Heavy lift/crane vessels must have special arrangements for ballasting and de-ballasting during lifting operations. This is to ensure stability during the operations.

12. **What role does an accommodation vessel play in offshore industry?**

    The accommodation vessels/barges are mainly to provide accommodation to workers on the adjacent rig/vessel/ facility. Sometimes the accommodations may not be enough and sometimes it is not safe for the people to stay there, so accommodation barges are positioned nearby.

13. What is the DP class of an Accommodation vessel?

An accommodation vessel may be DP class 2 or class 3. When the vessel is connected to a rig or production facility with a gangway, it is usually a DP class 3 vessel. When outside 500-meter zone the accommodation vessel may be a DP class 2 vessel.

14. What is drilling vessel's main role?

A drilling ship/vessel is mainly used for carrying out drilling operations. Some drilling vessels may also be used for maintenance and completion activities of the existing oil well. The figure below shows a drill ship, connected to a riser system carrying out drilling activity. .

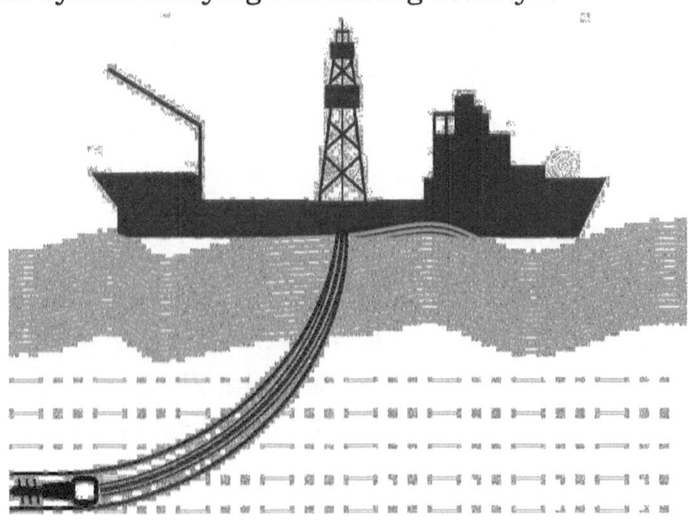

Fig: 5.3　Drill Ship

15. What is mobile drilling offshore unit (MODU)?

A drilling vessel may be also called a MODU. These vessels could be bottom standing, sometime self-elevating, moored or on DP. Mostly the safety requirements dictate DP drilling operations.

16. What are the risks involved into drilling operations?

    Drilling activities are very safety critical operations. Care must be taken at all stages of operations to ensure that injury to people onboard and in the near vicinity must be avoided. Also important is ensuring safety of riser system, nearby assets (on surface and in the subsea) and the environmental pollution. So, carrying out these operations using DP system make better sense.

17. What is floating production storage and offloading (FPSO) vessel?

    A FPSO is used for both the production as well as storage activities. This stored produce must be offloaded to a shuttle tanker or to a pipeline. Most FPSOs are either DP 2 or DP class 3 vessels. Some old FPSO may be even a DP class 1 vessel. DP system helps FPSO to maintain the riser angle, using the riser angle management system (RAMS).

18. What is a DP shuttle tanker?

    A shuttle tanker is usually a DP class 2/3 DP enabled vessel which shuttle between shore and offshore to offload the oil produced by the FPSO. Both the FPSO and the shuttle tanker use a special mode of DP called "weathervane" mode.

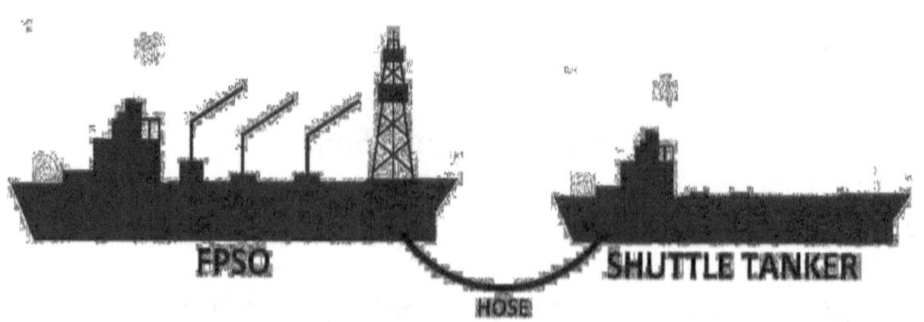

Fig: 5.4 DP Shuttle Tanker and FPSO

19. What is a trenching vessel?

    A trenching vessel is used to dig trenches on the subsea surface so that the cables or the pipelines be buried for safety purposes. This is done to endure that the pipeline and cables are safe from the mechanical damages.

20. What is recommended class of DP for a Trenching vessel?

    A DP Trenching vessel may be either DP class 2 or 3. However some old vessels are DP class 1 engaged in these activities.

21. What is jack up vessel used in offshore industry?

    A jack up vessel may be used for some special applications such as wind service. May use three or more legs to provide stabilised and safe operations in economical way. IMCA recommends either a DP 2 or DP 3 class of vessel for such operations.

22. What are offshore supply vessel's main tasks?

    Offshore supply vessel or OSV are used for logistic purposes in the offshore industry. There may be different classes of DP depending upon the regions, types of supplies and size of the vessel.

23. What is an Anchor handling Vessel?

    An anchor handling vessel is used for anchor handling of the offshore installations. An AHV or AHTS, as they are commonly known as, may be a DP 1/2/3 as per the requirements.

24. What is a Well Stimulation Vessel?

    A well stimulation vessel is used to help in offshore intervention by enhancing the oil well productivity. These vessels may be fitted with various chemical tanks and make use of blenders and then high-pressure chemicals are injected into the well to stimulate for better productivity.

25. What a Rock Dumper or Rock Placement Vessel?

A rock dumping vessel is used to cover the trenched pipeline or cables with rocks for safety purposes. A very technological advanced vessel may also make use of ROV assisted rock dumping operations.

26. What is the purpose of a DP Dredging Vessel?

The dredgers are used to dredge out a particular area. So, the accuracy of dredging operations may be enhanced by using DP assisted dredging. The class of the vessel may depend upon the type of dredging operations accuracy requirements. IMCA recommends that depending on the operations, a dredger may be classed as DP 1/2/3

27. What is a Service Operations Vessel?

A Service Operations Vessel or SOV is used mainly to provide support windmill area. These vessels may have the kind of onboard workshops required for the purpose. Some of these vessels may additionally have accommodation for the personnel deployed for windmill installation etc.

CHAPTER 6

DP CLASS OR EQUIPMENT CLASS BASED ON IMO-MSC 645 AND 1580

1. Does a class 3 DP vessel always have to be fully redundant??

   No, there may be non-redundant arrangements of connections between separate and redundant systems. This special arrangement is provided and properly documented as per provisions as given in IMO/MSC/645 para 3.1.3/3.2.4, with the main purpose of providing safety.

2. How should the switch-over to the back-up control system for equipment class 3 should be arranged?

   The changeover is needed in case the main DP system has failed and then the DP operator decides to change over to the back up control. So, as per the IMO/MSC/645 the changeover must be fitted on the main DP controls and must be changed over manually when need arises.

3. Classification Societies require a Power Management System for which class of DP vessels?

   DP class 3 or 2 require power management system to be installed. As power management helps a great way, most of the vessels are installed with PMS.

4. What is Equipment Class 1 or DP class 1?

In an equipment Class 1 or DP class loss of position is likely to happen once there is a single point failure. This is due to the fact that there is no redundancy provided or there is single redundancy. This the most basic DP system available in the market.

5. What is Equipment Class 2 or DP class 2?

DP systems designed to be classed as DP class 2 should have dual redundancy.

This helps the vessel to maintain her position in the event of a single point failure. The remaining redundancy (after single point failure) will provide support and thereby vessel maintaining her position.

6. What is Equipment Class 3 or DP class 3?

DP class 3 or equipment Class 3 is designed to also withstand flooding or fire, as one set of redundancy is installed in a A/60 bulkhead isolated compartment. This arrangement is unique to a DP class 3. Fire or flood in any one compartment without the system failing, so one set of equipment is installed in a fire/flood proof compartment (separated by A/60 bulkhead). Loss of position is not expected to happen when a single failure which may include loss of compartment due to fire or flooding and losing out the redundancy installed in that compartment.

7. What is DP class 0 (Equipment class Zero)?

Though, this class is not recognized by the authorities (IMO), certain classification societies have recognized as a system with which has capacity of thruster manual control and also has the possibility of heading control automatically.

ABS class recognizes this system as DPS-0 notation, LRS DP Class recognizes this as DP (CM) and the DNV recognizes DP class 0 as DYNPOS-AUTS.

8. What are new requirements for an automatic power management system (PMS) for various DP classes as per the new guidelines IMO MSC 1580?

    The new guidelines mandate to have at least power management system (PMS) be installed on DP classes 2 and 3 vessels. This makes the vessel with more redundant and safer for the operations by increasing the reliability. The main function of power management system is to ensure the availability of electrical power by avoiding black out. The PMS may be semi-automatic or automatic and its integration and sophistications deployed.

9. Which class of DP vessel requires FMEA?

    As per IMO/MSC 645 and IMO/MSC/1580 a DP class 2 and DP class 3 vessels will have to comply to the FMEA requirements as promulgated in the referred IMO guidelines. The results of FMEA proving trials must be maintained and stored onboard. The FMEA must be maintained current by regular updates and by conducting annual FMEA trials. The FMEA process may defined as the systematic analysis of the DP system with an aim so as to prove that when a single failure occurs, it will not result in the loss of position or heading or both.

10. What are the standard constituents of a DP class 1 system?

    A standard DP class 1 system may consist of minimum one operator station fitted in the bridge console; the required number of environmental sensors, at least two reference sensors and one DP controller suitably located with required input output devices. Both the position reference must not be of the same type to avoid common mode of failure.

11. What are the standard constituents of a DP class 2 system?

DP equipment class 2 has dual redundancy, sometimes referred to as dual redundant system. The dual redundancy has an advantage over the single redundancy that a single worst-case failure may not result into a loss of ships heading or position or both. If there is a loss of one or more of the active components like thrusters, related remote controlled valves, generators, switchboards etc. may not result into a failure and thereby losing heading or position or both.

12. What are the standard constituents of a DP Class 3 system?

A DP Class 3 must have triple redundancy and one set of redundant equipment must be installed in A/60 bulkhead area. A/60 area can withstand fire or flooding for at least 60 minutes and thus in such eventuality, the system may be utilised to move the vessel to safe place ensuring safety of own vessel and that of others in vicinity.

13. Discuss the electrical power system for a DP class 1 vessel.

Electrical system onboard a DP class 1 vessel is a non-redundant system with one switchboard and no bus tie breaker. The electrical distribution system is also non redundant and old vessel may not have a power management system but vessel following IMO MSC letter 1580 (June, 2017 onwards), will have a power management system

14. Discuss the electrical power system for a DP class 2 vessel.

DP 2 vessel electrical power system is designed to be redundant with two switch boards and a bust tie breaker to connect/disconnect the switchboards. DP 2 vessel power distribution systems is designed to be redundant so as to avoid single point failure. Redundancy of power is designed to be monitored and controlled by an automatic or semi-automatic PMS.

15. Discuss the electrical power system for a DP class 3 vessel.

   A DP class 3 electrical power system is redundant in technical design and physical separation, (separate compartments A-60 bulkhead). Main switchboards also will be arranged in two separate compartments for safety and redundancy purpose. The bus tie breaker is expected to be accommodated in each switch board and provision of power management system,

16. What are the thruster requirements for the various DP class of vessels?

   Arrangement of thrusters for DP class 1 is non redundant, whereas the DP vessel class 2 and class 3, thruster system installed is designed to be redundant. DP class 2 vessel will have thrusters' redundancy in technical design, whereas a DP class 3 vessel will have redundancy in technical design and physical separation in A-60 bulkhead. Single levers for each thruster at main DP-control centre is a requirement for all the DP classes.

17. What are the requirements for the various DP class vessels for uninterruptible power source (UPS)?

   A DP class 1 will have at least one UPS, DP class 2 vessel are to be fitted with two UPS ensuring redundancy. Whereas the redundancy requirements for a DP class 3 is met by having three UPS, one of the UPS being installed in a separate compartment.

18. What is the requirement for position reference sensors (PRS) for a DP class 1?

All DP class 1 vessels are required to have at least two PRS. To ensure safety, both the PRS are not supposed to chosen which work on the same principle. For example, installing two DGPS doesn't meet the requirements of a DP class 1 vessel. The two PRS must be working on two different principles thereby avoiding common mode of failure of PRS.

CHAPTER 7
BASICS OF ELECTRICAL PROPULSION AND THRUSTERS

1. **What is Thruster system?**

    Thruster system include all components and sub systems which together make it possible to supply the DP system with necessary thrust force in the required direction.

2. **What does thruster system include?**

    Every thruster must have a prime mover and its auxiliary systems which may include pipeline for cooling etc. Then to control thrusters it is necessary to have thruster control electronics, manual control lever for each thruster, and associated cables and the cable route.

3. **What is the minimum number of thrusters required for DP Classes 2 vessel?**

    A DP 2 vessel requires redundancy as per the IMO/MSC/645 or 1580. The general practice in the current market is that a DP 2 vessel may have two bow thrusters and two stern thrusters assisted by a bow/mid thruster and thereby providing redundancy.

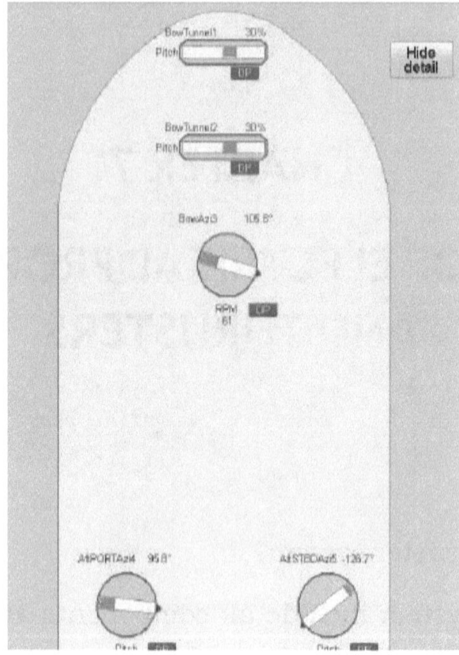

Fig: 7.1 Minimum Number of Thrusters–DP 2– Courtesy Kongsberg

4. Explain "Thruster Biasing"? Where is it applied?

Thruster biasing is one of the settings for the thrusters used in DP. Thruster biasing is activated to avoid unnecessary azimuth movement of thrusters. This may happen during low weather conditions and hence a pair of thrusters may be set in biasing mode.

Fig: 7.2 Thruster Biasing

5. What is thruster exclusion zone or thruster barred zone?

A range of those sectors/angles of azimuth wherein the output of thruster will be reduced to zero or minimum possible using RPM or pitch control as applicable. This is done to minimise the disturbance caused by the thruster wash of one thruster on the other thruster. Barred zone settings may also be applied to an azimuth thruster which may cause disturbance to a position reference sensor or ROV/diver launching stations during such operations.

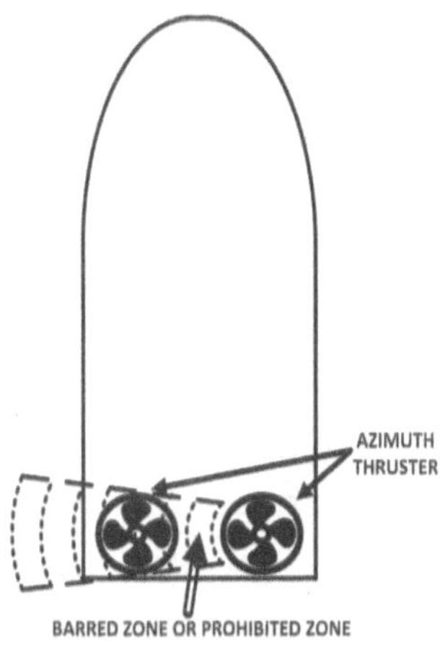

Fig: 7.3 Thruster Barred Zone/Prohibited Zone

6. When a tunnel thruster may become ineffective?

A tunnel thruster may become ineffective if the vessel makes a movement at a speed more than three knots. Also, in some cases when the tunnel is too long the reflected force from the tunnel walls may affect the thrusters.

7. What is Prohibited zone for a thruster?

Prohibited zone is created so as to prevent azimuth thrusters from interfering with each other, that means the wash from one thruster will disturb the other one.

8. When the thrusters on a DP vessel may become ineffective?

When another vessel is working in the close proximity, and the thruster of that vessel may throw the thruster wash on this vessel, the thrusters are likely to be less effective. Usually under such circumstances the "current"/"DP Current" or "Residual as Current" may increase. The DPO must keep observing such unexpected increase in the DP current.

9.   How would you define an azimuth thruster?

Azimuth thrusters, as the name applies, are those thrusters which can rotate 360 degrees and thus do not require a rudder.

10.   What is "Ready" signal for a thruster?

Thruster ready signal is sent from thruster controls to the DP controller indicating that the thruster is ready to be enabled on DP. When thruster is running and if any of the safety conditions are not fulfilled, the thruster ready signal will not be generated. Ready signal is a digital input signal.

11.   What is "Running" signal for a thruster?

When a thruster is running a signal is sent to the DP controller that the thruster is now running. The thruster running signal is a digital input signal. Thruster running signal is a prerequisite for thruster ready signal.

12.   What is "Enabled" signal for a thruster?

Once a thruster is running, and all safeties in good condition, the operator on bridge may enable the thruster by click of a button on the panel or from the menu. Now the thruster is enabled and is under the control of DP.

13.   What is "Command" or "Set point" signal for a thruster?

The set point or command signal is generated from the controller with the help of a signal. This signal is called analog signal. Older vessels the signal could be +/- 10 Volt and now for the new vessel this signal is 4-20 mA signal.

14. What is "Feedback" signal for a thruster?

Feedback signal is generated by the thruster after it has reached the commanded situation. For an example if a bow thruster set point was set to 50% stbd. (Command set to 50% Stbd.), thruster will start applying thrust and when it attains 50%, a signal is generated from thruster to the DP controller that the required thrust is attained. The signal could be a +/- 10 V or 4-20mA.

15. What are the expected design criteria for the Failure of Thruster System?

As per the standard design criteria, all thrusters should be designed in such a way that any failure must not result in the thruster rotate or go to uncontrolled full pitch and speed. If a failure happens, for example a pitch failure, the design will help the pitch to freeze or come back to zero pitch and not fail to a full pitch in either direction.

16. Explain what is Fixed Pitch Propeller (FPP) thruster?

The pitch is fixed, and the speed is controlled either by a silicon-controlled rectifier (SCR) - controlled DC motor or frequency-controlled AC motor.

17. Explain how thrust is controlled?

Thrust may be controlled either by controlling the speed (RPM) of a motor or by controlling pitch of the blade of the thrusters. Usually smaller thrusters utilize pitch control method and heavy thrusters use RPM control.

18. What is Thruster Allocation Logic or TAL?

Thruster Allocation Logic or TAL is the output of the DP controller. This defines which thrusters will work to provide the required thrust so that the vessel maintains her position.

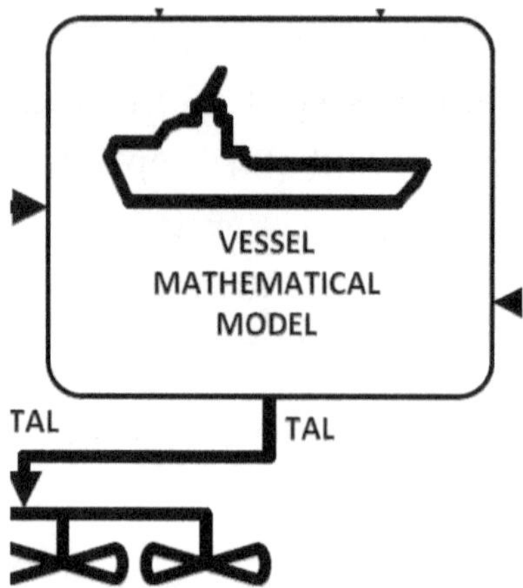

Fig: 7.4   Thruster Allocation Logic (TAL) – The output from DP Controller

19. Explain what are the types of thruster available in DP market?

Broadly, thrusters may be divided into two categories. One those thrusters which are used for station keeping only. Two, those thrusters which may be used for station keeping, and low-speed propulsion, i.e. depending on their capacity and design, these thrusters may assist in a transit speed of between 6-8 knots and 12-14 knots respectively,

20. Name the various ways controllable pitch propeller (CPP) failures may occur?

CPP failure may occur due to:

•   Loss of hydraulic fluid

•   Failure of control valve

- Mechanical failure

- Feedback failure

21. What is Fail Safe Mode of thrusters?

When a failure happens, the controls try to maintain the output to the nearest possible of the point at which it failed. For an example, the "Fail-safe" mode for controllable pitch propellers in DP vessels is the "zero pitch". This means that when a failure of this thruster happens, it is expected to go to zero pitch, means no output from this thruster. The loss of thrust will be complimented by the other thrusters online.

22. What the DPO should do if he/she observes a CPP thruster has failed to full pitch?

A careful DPO will be able to make out the failed thruster by looking at the command and feedback page. If there is a wide gap between the command and the feedback, this indicates that thruster has failed. The most appropriate action should be that the operators identifies the failed thruster and emergency stop is activated.

23. What is Thruster Allocation Logic or Thruster Transform?

TAL or thruster transform may be defined as DP control system algorithm which calculates the required demand for each thruster to achieve the DP controller's output for surge sway and yaw motion control of the ship.

24. What is the minimum rate of turn for azimuth rotation of an Azimuth thruster?

The generally acceptable time for a full rotation of azimuth is 30 seconds for 360 degrees.

25. What affects the amount of thruster force used while maintaining station in the auto-position mode?

    The environmental forces acting on the vessel and excursion from set point, if any, will determine the input to the controller, which in turn will calculate the amount of thrust required which is commonly known as thruster allocation logic (TAL).

26. What is the approximate force available from a DP azimuth thruster, which is going "astern" direction?

    There is no definite figure which may be claimed but while an azimuth thruster is working astern, it is observed that it may not give 100% thrust. The thrust is generally limited between 75-95%.

27. What is an "Azimuth" thruster?

    An azimuth thruster may be defined as a thruster which is capable of providing 360 degrees directional control of thrust.

28. What is a "Thruster Exclusion Zone"?

    "Thruster Exclusion Zone" or barred zones are those sectors of azimuth wherein the thrust is reduced to bare minimum or to zero for safety reasons for each thruster or keeping a position reference sensor safe from noise/disturbance. This may also be applied to certain operations like launching of ROV or divers.

29. A Thruster may malfunction during operation due to some fault conditions. What is best way to detect a faulty thruster?

    DP professional must be familiar with the signals of thruster. The thruster makes use of thruster command and feedback signals for this purpose. If there is wide gap between the command and feedback signals, it means that the thruster has failed. The most appropriate action would be to activate the emergency stop for this failed thruster.

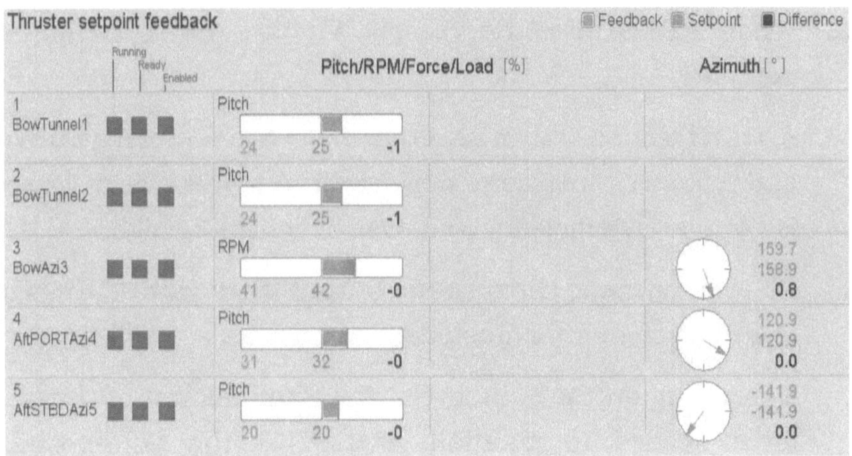

Fig: 7.5   Thruster Setpoint (Command) and Feedback Signals – Courtesy Kongsberg

It is important to note here that if there is difference in the set point and feedback, it may be inferenced that there is a problem with this thruster. Most DP systems show this in a different color for easy detection by the operator.

30. A DP 3 vessel is fitted with three azimuth thrusters at the bow and three azimuth thrusters at the stern. The thruster menu has 'Fixed Azimuth' mode. When may this mode be used?

The identified pair of thrusters may be set to "fixed mode" or "Biasing mode" when the thrusters are continuously rotation(hunting) may be due to very low weather conditions.

31. What affects the performance of tunnel thrusters?

As tunnel thrusters are fitted inside a tunnel, a number of factors affect the performance, such as rough seas, high speed of vessel and proximity of a nearby platform/ structure/vessel. A long tunnel may also reflect water and affect the performance.

32. What is Diesel Electric Vessel? Why are they becoming so popular?

A vessel will be known as a diesel electric vessel if all drives and thrusters are electrically driven. Yes, this type of vessels is popular as efficiency and ease of control is high.

33. What happens to the thruster output when gain settings on the DP system are adjusted?

Depending on the gain levels, the total amount of thruster force needed to maintain station in the auto-position mode may vary. High gain may require a greater number of thruster and thrust level may shoot up in the currently enabled thrusters.

34. What is requirement as per IMO/MSC 1580 for thruster remote control?

Each thruster on a DP system should be capable of being remote-controlled individually, independently of the DP control system.

35. As per IMO/MSC 1580, what is the new requirement for thruster emergency stop?

Individual thruster emergency stop systems should be arranged in the DP control station.

36. What are the two major factors that the azimuth thrusters face and their performance is adversely affected?

The performance of azimuth thrusters may be affected badly by the interaction of the thruster wash with the ship's hull or other structure/s. Secondly the thruster wash of one thruster may affect the other thruster adversely and performances may be degraded.

37. What is the best way to identify a failed or faulty thruster?

A faulty thruster may best be identified by having a look at the command and feedback. If there is a gap between the command and feedback, it indicates that the thruster is either sluggish or has failed.

38. Name two methods of controlling thrust on board a DP vessel.

The thrust may be controlled by a) Pitch control and b) RPM control. In Pitch control method the blade angle is controlled by using hydraulics. In the RPM control methods, the system utilizes ways to control thrust by regulating the speed. Variable frequency drive (VFD) is one such popular method.

39. What are the main features of an azimuth thruster?

Azimuth thruster has the following main features.

- Can rotate 360 degrees

- May be pitch controlled or RPM controlled

- May have nozzle arrangement

- May be fixed or retrievable

- Can function as ships main propulsion

- Dangers of grounding as hanging below the vessel

40. What may cause a thruster to fail?

The general causes of a thruster failure are as below.

- Grounding damages

- Rope fouling

- Contact with hardware kept below

- Failure of hydraulic system

- Failure of seals etc.

- Bearing damage

- Gear problems

- Feedback problem

- Mechanical linkage disengage/broken

41. What is best action when the DP operator observes a thruster runs away on full pitch?

The DP operator must be able to identify the failed thruster and activate emergency stop to the failed thruster. If this is not done with in approximately 20 seconds, it is highly unlikely that the vessel may continue to hold position.

42. Why is it advisable to start the CPP thrusters in "zero pitch"?

Controllable pitch propellers are expected to be started while the pitch is at zero. This to avoid excessive use of power, resulting into heavy thrust and uncontrolled move. This is considered as an unsafe act and may result into loss of position and blackout. Appropriate measures are incorporated in the controls of such thrusters that they are started only in zero pitch.

43. What is meaning of thruster modulation?

Thruster modulation is experienced when there are a significant and frequent changes in the thruster load.

44. What is so special about a fixed pitch variable speed thruster?

For a FPP and variable speed thruster which may draw small currents when started, less power used at small thrust requirements and these may be designed to shut down when a failure in control systems is detected.

45. How is pitch reduction function tested for a CPP thruster?

Most DP systems have the pitch reduction function for safeguarding power system from overloading. This function may be tested by moving the vessel in all directions including heading simultaneously. If Azimuths thrusters are used, biasing may be applied. When the power limit approaches the set value (Approximately 80%), warning and alarms may be observed. The DP system software will bring the RPM for the RPM controlled thrusters down and reduce the pitch of the CPP thrusters.

46. How is thruster emergency stop switch tested?

It is important to test the emergency stop switches for the thrusters and records are maintained. To test the emergency, stop switch, operate the switch and observe that the thruster is stopped, deselected from DP

47. What is procedure to check the failure of thruster ready signals?

Thruster ready signals are tested by disconnecting the thruster ready signal. Properly identify the connections at the input/output devices at the controller and observe the thruster not ready indication. Some systems may have block whereas other may have a tick mark to represent the ready signal.

48. How is the thruster command/feedback signal checked?

    The thruster command and feedback signal may be checked at the two places. Firstly, at the thruster control panel which may be known as field station or field devices, secondly on the DP controller input/output devices. By referring the circuit diagram, the location of the wires carrying these signals may be verified. These signals are either +/- 10 volt or 4-20 mA, are referred to as analog signals. The same applies to the azimuth angle command and feedback signals also.

49. How is fail safe arranged in DP thrusters?

    As pert the existing rules and guidelines available, the DP thrusters must be provided with a failsafe facility. Such conditions may include as below.

    - Failing as set or commanded

    - Failing to zero command/zero thrust

CHAPTER 8

POWER, POWER MANAGEMENT SYSTEM AND UNINTERRUPTIBLE POWER SUPPLY

1. What is the status of bus tie breaker during Class 3 DP Operations?

   The status of bus tie breakers during DP class 3 operations are as per the guidelines provided in IMO/MSC/645 para 3.1.3 and para 3.2.4. These guidelines explain that full redundancy may not always be possible for DP class 3 operations. In such a situation a redundant system must not be affected by a single failure on in one system.

2. What is power system of a DP vessel?

   Power system of a DP enabled vessels may be defined have various parts or sub systems which together can work and supply the required electrical power to the DP system. The power system may include the following but not limited to-

   a) Prime movers

   b) Alternators or Generators

   c) Main Switchboards or "Bus" as they are commonly referred to as.

d) Power Distribution (including cables and the route cables follow)

e) Uninterruptible power supplies (UPS)

f) A suitable Power management system

3. What do you understand by the prime movers in the power system of a DP vessel?

Prime movers, generally diesel engines, the associated auxiliary systems which may include the piping arrangements, cooling system, fuel system, lubrication (including pre-lubrication). The system also includes hydraulics, pneumatic system and preheating as required.

4. Explain what is spinning reserve?

Spinning reserve may be defined as the difference between online generator capacity and consumed power. Most DP systems display this on a page on DP controls station.

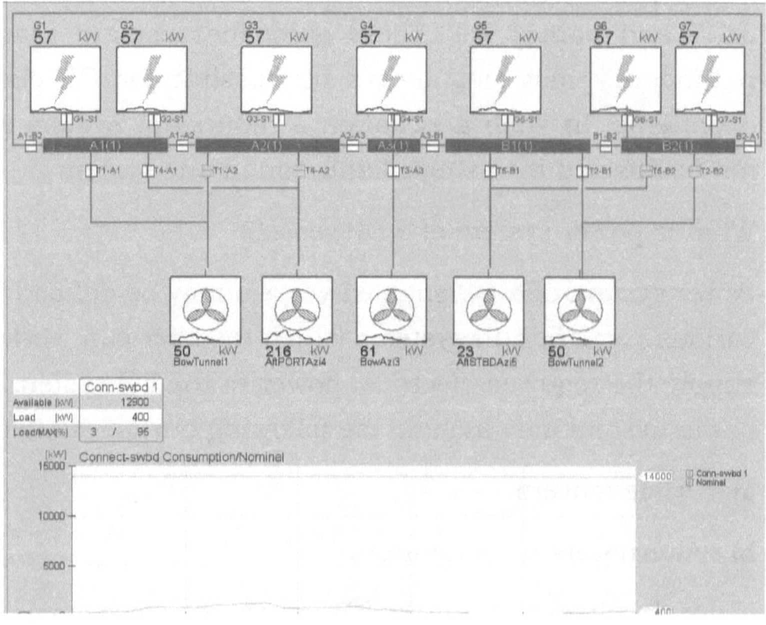

Fig: 8.1 Spinning Reserve (Courtesy Kongsberg)

5. What is power management system?

    The power management system or PMS may be defined as a computer-based system, which can operate with both open and closed bus-tie breakers where applicable for a DP 2 or DP 3 vessel. PMS may be a standalone system capable of controlling power of a DP vessel or it may be integrated with the complete automation of the vessel depending upon the level of integration.

6. Name four different failure modes which may cause backout.

    Depending upon the type and design of vessel these may vary. The four failure are as below.

    1. Governor failure

    2. AVR failure

    3. Short circuit and circuit bus tie(s) fail to open due to a hidden fault

    4. There may be insufficient capacity after a worst-case failure as the DP control system immediately increases the load on the remaining thrusters and thereby generators and one of them trips on overload.

7. What may cause a blackout on DP vessel while the bus tie(s) may be open or closed bus?

    After a worst-case failure, there is not enough power available. This is due to the fact that the DP control system quickly increases the load on the remaining thrusters as per the TAL. Increased load on the thrusters will make the generators heavily loaded and may be a black out.

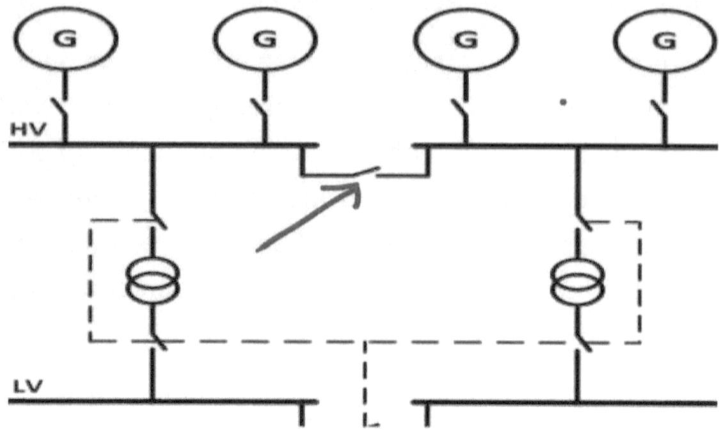

Fig: 8.2   Bus Tie Breaker

8.   How is the DP control system protected against fluctuations and failures in main power?

The protection of DP control system against main power fluctuations and failures is done by connecting the DP control system with an uninterruptible power supply (UPS).

9.   What is the main purpose of UPS?

The main purpose of the UPS is to supply power which is free from fluctuations and interruptions. UPS is powered from the secondary source. In case of the primary source failing, the secondary source must be able to feed the power for the continued operation of the equipment.

10. What is minimum time is expected to last the UPS supply?

All battery powered UPS are expected to supply power for minimum of 30 minutes. Though in reality, the UPS and its batteries may much more capable.

Fig: 8.3 Uninterruptible Power Supply (UPS).

11. One of the functions of power management system is to continually monitor the available power on board. Which power are we referring to here?

    The available power to be monitored by the PMS is called by various names such as "spinning reserve" or "Reserve Power". The reserve power or the spinning reserve is the available power without starting any standby generator.

12. How many kilo watts are equivalent to a horsepower?

    746 W or.746kW is equivalent power to one horsepower. Or 1.34 HP is equal to one Kilowatt.

13. What are the probable actions a power management system may initiate to ensure that switchboard is not overloaded?

    The PMS may initiate load dependent start of standby diesel generators. In case of all generators already running, load shedding may be initiated (Preferential Tripping). Phase back of some thruster till power is available

14. Which type of failure mode may cause a blackout on DP vessel not considering its bus tie(s) are open or closed bus?

    Any failure which have reduced the power capacity to such a level that when the DP control system allocates thrust to the online thruster and immediately thrust will go up and hence the power consumption. This may result into blackout.

15. Name the probable failures that may cause a blackout even though the vessels' power system may be configured as "Closed Bus Tie".

    The following failures may result into a black even if the vessels power plant is working in closed bus tie condition.

    a) Governor failure

    b) AVR failure

    c) Short circuit

    d) Bus tie failure (failed to open)

    e) Insufficient capacity after some failure

16. How a DP control system (processors, displays and consoles) is protected against a main power failure or fluctuations of the ship's AC power supply?

    It is especially important to supply the DP controls with a stabilized power source. If this may not be possible then the only options to connect the DP control to an alternate source of power i.e. uninterruptible power supply (UPS).

17. Can a DP 2 vessels with two switchboards operate only with generators connected on one switchboard with bus tie breaker closed?

    No, because the loss of the switchboard with all generators connected would cause a total blackout. The purpose of all these arrangements for a DP 2 vessel is for ensuring redundancy.

18. Why is it safer to operate a DP vessel power system with an open bus tie breaker?

An open bus tie breaker provides redundancy and hence safety against complete or full blackout. A bus tie also helps in isolating an electrical fault like shorting or grounding in one section of the main switchboards.

19. Why does a DP vessel require power management system with preferential tripping?

DP vessels are particularly vulnerable to power shortages and blackout conditions due to frequently fluctuating power requirements. To provide safety against these variations, against all DP vessels with Class 2 and class 3 must be installed with a power management system with preferential tripping arrangements. Preferential trip will disconnect unimportant consumers to ensure power is supplied to the required thrusters.

20. What is the arrangement for the DP system to get power from UPS when mains fail?

According to IMO MSC/Circ. 645 of 1994, an uninterruptible power supply (UPS) battery system should be able to power up the DP control system following a mains supply failure for minimum period of 30 minutes.

21. For a DP 2 vessel, prior to entering the 500-meter zone, how should the vessel power management system (PMS) be setup?

PMS is to be setup with main bus tie breaker in open condition, unless as per FMEA some special arrangements are in place and tested.

22. What is reserve of power at any given time?

A function of the Power Management System is to continually monitor 'Available Power'.

'Available Power' is the power available from the generators online. This also called as spinning reserve, because of the fact that the power supplied by generators which are "spinning" after subtracting the power which is used.

23. How is UPS tested for DP controls?

UPS for DP controls may be tested by switching off input power to UPS (220V). The battery output should be checked for a maximum 30 minutes. UPS may be tested by disconnecting the output line to observe UPS failure alarm. All services fed from this UPS may go off and must be observed carefully. Make sure all supplies are reconnected and equipment restarted on completion of the test.

24. How is the failure of battery chargers for 24V DC systems and failure of the Low Power system (LP System) tested?

The low power and battery charger failure may be tested by switching off the required input breaker. Observe that the battery charger stops functioning and the alarm gets activated accordingly. The battery must be able to feed the connected services for more than 30 minutes as tested during FMEA trials.

25. How is main switchboard bus bar failure tested?

Main switchboard bus bar/s failure may be tested by disconnecting all the generators connected to it and ensuing that the bustie breaker is open. Observe that the services fed by the bus are off and alarms observed as well. These may be already recorded in the FMEA trials.

26. How to check the standby start of the air compressor?

    The purpose is to check if the standby compressor comes on once the online compressor is gone off. This can be tested by switching off the main (leading) compressor. Allow system to drain so that the standby system may cut in. It is important to note here that the standby compressor must start before the low-pressure alarm is activated.

27. What are the main reasons of increased load on the switchboard?

    The following may cause sudden or gradual increase in the load.

    - Environmental conditions change like squall, gusts and solitons etc.

    - Use of unjustified DP joysticks

    - Position jumps due to weather (drive offs)

    - Hotel/accommodation loads

    - Sudden change of heading or position or both the movements together

    - A failed thruster

28. How is it planned to avoid making power management system (PMS) a common failure point?

    By ensuring that PMS itself doesn't become a common failure point the following precautions may be incorporated.

    - Limiting PMS functions to generator management activities.

    - Blackout avoidance and blackout recovery functions

29. How is the bustie arrangement in a DP class 3 vessel power system?

    A DP class 3 vessel power system must include redundant bustie breakers. The bustie breakers must be able to operate safely in case of fire or flooding and ensuing safety by activating automatically.

30. What is a single line diagram for a power system?

    The power distribution system consists of certain bus sections located in the Engine Control Room plus the emergency switchboard. The power system is operated as two electrically independent systems with the emergency switchboard being powered from designated power system in normal operation.

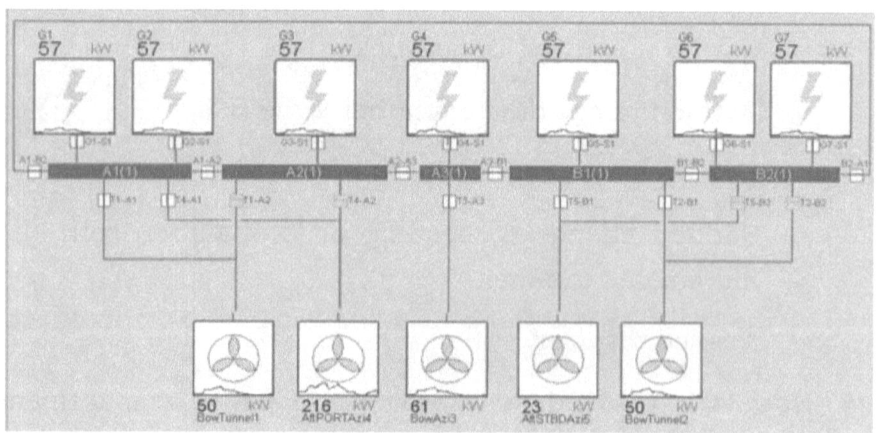

Fig: 8.4   Power Single Line Diagram (Courtesy Kongsberg)

CHAPTER 9

ENVIRONMENTAL SENSORS

1. What is the purpose of a Vertical Reference Unit (VRU) or Vertical Reference Sensor (VRS)?

    The VRU/VRS or the motion reference unit (MRU) measure the pitch, roll (and heave) motions of the floating structure. VRU measures roll and pitch and MRU measure all three i.e. roll, pitch and heave.

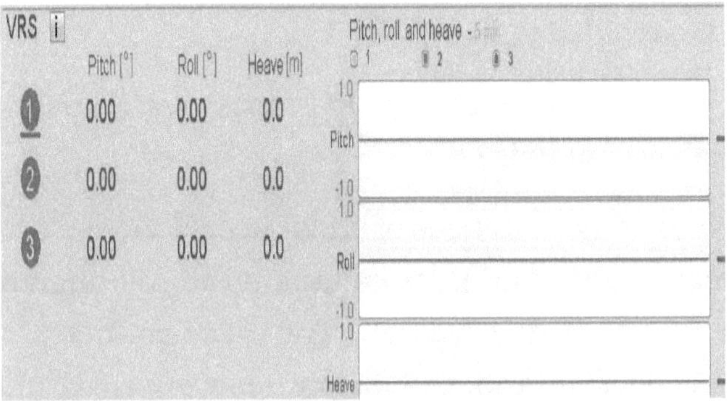

Fig: 9.1   VRS/VRU/MRU – Preference to VRS 1 (Courtesy Kongsberg)

2. What single sensor or component is the most essential part of the DP system?

    The DP system is consisting of seven components. All are important but among the sensors (the environmental sensors) the gyro is the most important one, as the gyro input is needed for almost all other sensors of DP. This makes the gyro as the most important sensor of DP system.

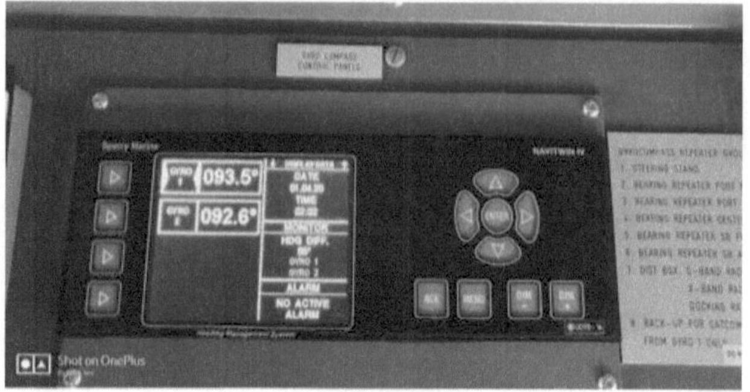

Fig: 9.2　Gyro

3. Why do we use VRU/MRU?

    VRU/VRS/MRU is used to measure the ships movements around the vertical axis, namely roll pitch and heave. Once these motions are measured, these are used to compensate the roll and pitch movements for the position reference sensors, so that the unnecessary movement of the vessel may be avoided.

4. How does the VRS/MRU/VRU measures ships movements on the vertical axis?

    A modern-day MRU uses of linear accelerometers to measure the movements and thus calculate the roll pitch and heave movements of the vessel. The accelerometers are very precise devices and can measure even small movements accurately.

5. What does a wind sensor measure? What is use of the wind sensor data?

    A wind sensor measures the speed and direction of the wind. The vessel is affected by the wind force. If the vessel must stay in position, it is necessary that the wind force and its direction to be measured and compensated for. In the figure below, all wind sensors are Ok and enabled but preference is given to wind sensor #2.

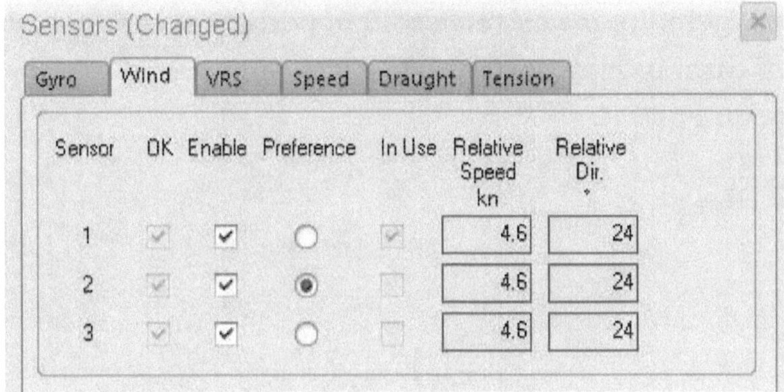

Fig: **9.3**   Wind Sensor– Courtesy Kongsberg

6. What is wind feed forward? What is the need for wind feed forward?

The wind feed-forward is a process wherein the measured wind is directly fed into the controller so that an immediate equal and opposite force may be applied by using thruster forces and thereby maintain the vessel in position.

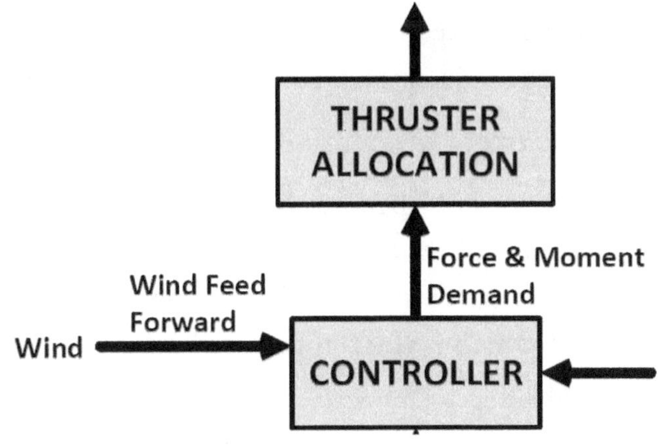

Fig: **9.4**   Wind feed Forward

7. What is rate of turn (ROT)? Name the device which measures it?

The speed at which the heading of the vessel is turning may be defined as the rate of turn (ROT). ROT is measured by the gyro. Its measurement id important as a very high rate of turning may require big thrust and hence big power to counteract it.

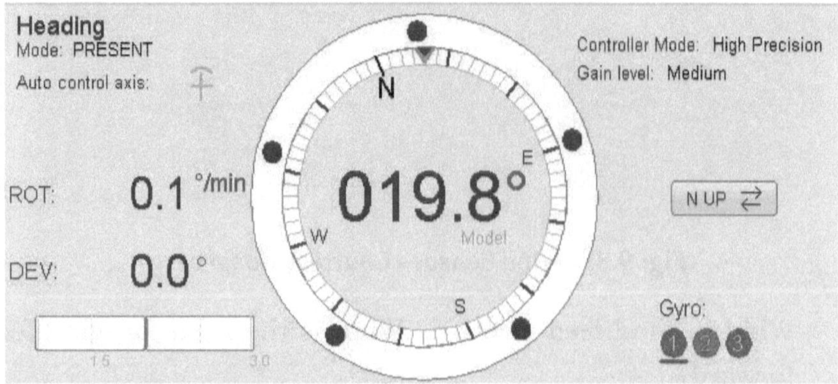

Fig: 9.5 Rate of turn (ROT) (Courtesy Kongsberg)

8. What may cause wind model errors?

One of the most common reason is locating the vessel in a position which is partly sheltered from the wind. This is due to the wind measured is not the same as acting on the windage area. This causes errors in the wind model.

9. How is DP current measured?

DP current is not measured but calculated. It has the history being called as current/DP Current/Residual as current. Most modern vessels now use the word "Residual as Current" which is the total sum of unknown forces acting on the vessel.'

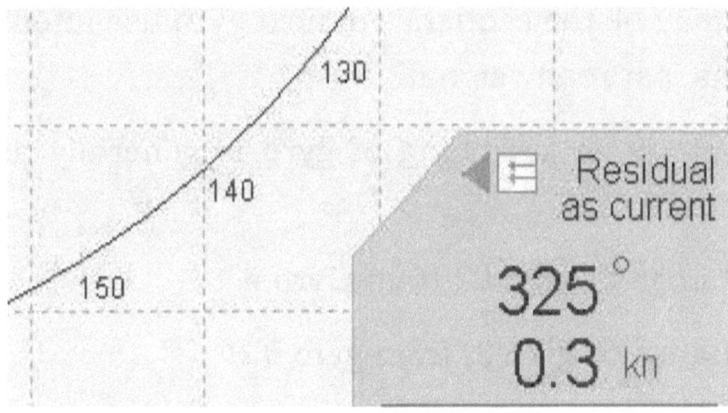

Fig: 9.6   DP Current/Residual as Current (Courtesy Kongsberg)

10. What is the purpose of a Vertical Reference Sensor input signal to the DP system?

    The purpose of vertical reference sensor is to measure roll and pitch of the vessel.

11. What happens when a "Gyro OK" or "Gyro Ready" signal is lost?

    In most DP systems, if the gyro selected as "Preferred" loses the OK signal the "next" gyro will be used.

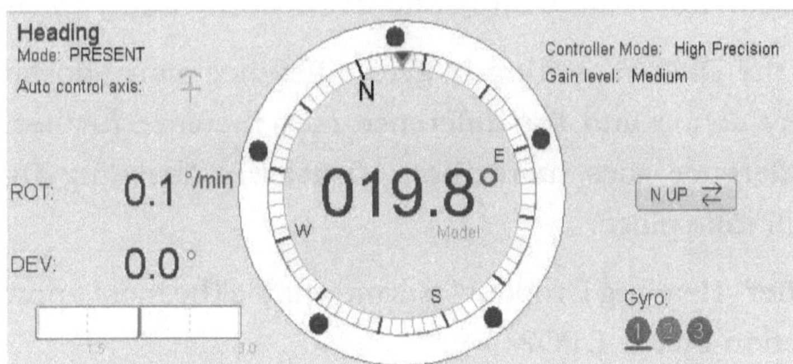

Fig: 9.7   Gyro OK/Ready Signal and Preference Gyro (Courtesy Kongsberg)

As shown above gyro #1 and #3 are ready and enabled (usually shown in green color. Gyro #2 is indicated by Red dot indicating not available/ready.

12. What may be the sequence of next gyro use after the gyro in use has lost ready signal?

    The automatic switching of gyro is generally arranged in this manner.

    - Change to gyro #2 from Gyro # 1

    - Change to gyro 3, from gyro #2

    - Change to Gyro 1. From gyro # 3

13. A DP vessel with two gyros, what is the significance of "Preferenced Gyro"?

    When only two gyros, the DP system will always use the Preferenced gyro. Usually "gyro Difference" alarm will get activated when the difference between the two gyros is exceeding 2 degrees. On getting the difference alarm, the DPO must decide which gyro to keep by comparing both gyros with the magnetic compass.

14. What happens if the DPO after getting Gyro Difference alarm, does not identify and deselect the faulty gyro?

    If the DPO on getting 2° gyro difference alarm doesn't take any action and the difference may increase further. If the difference goes more than 10 degrees "heading Dropout" will take place.

15. After "Heading Dropout" alarm, what is the most appropriate action by the DPO?

    To handle such a situation most of the DP system must be set to "Standby" mode. Standby mode is also considered as reset mode.

16. A DP vessel fitted with three gyros, what is the significance of "Preferenced Gyro"?

If a vessel is using three sensors and if one of them deviates more than 2° from the median that gyro will be rejected. If it is the "Preferenced" gyro which is rejected, then the DP system will switch to the median gyro. As a gyro is rejected, an alarm is activated.

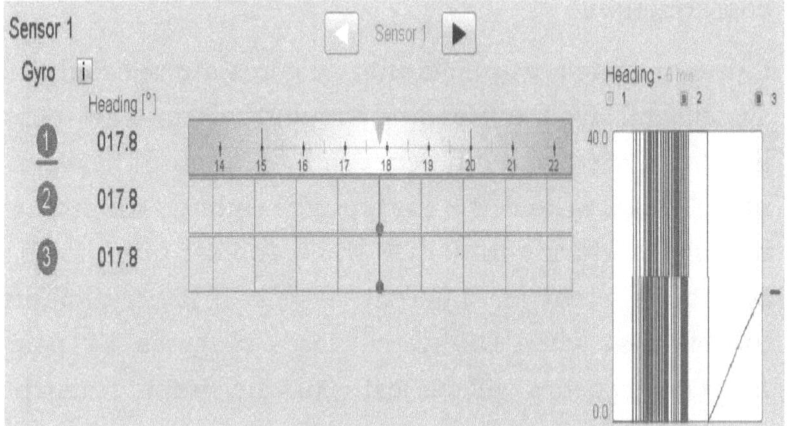

Fig: 9.8   Preference Gyro #1 (Courtesy Kongsberg)

An underscore below gyro #1 indicates that this gyro is now the preference gyro. The preference may be changed by the operator.

17. What is the significance of "Gyro rejected" message?

This message is reported if the difference between the value that is read from the sensor and the median value of all the enabled sensors of this type exceeds a limit (Usually 10 degrees). Once a gyro is rejected, the data from the sensor is not used by the DP system. This arrangement works only when at least three gyros are online.

18. What is Gyro Prediction Error?

    If there is a difference of more than 6° between the model and the measurement the sensor is rejected by the prediction test. The limit may be different for different vessels and is set between 4° to 10°. This message is given if two sensors are enabled.

19. What is "Heading Dropout" alarm? What are its consequences?

    If due to some reasons/faults, all gyros are rejected the DP system will give the "Heading Dropout" alarm. This message is given if there is a difference of more than 6° between the model heading and the measured heading. The limits are usually set during initial DP trials and set up process and may be different for different vessels. It is very important to note that when DP system loses all gyros, all position reference sensors will be lost. Position dropout alarm will get activated after 30 second.

20. What is the working principle of cup type wind sensor?

    The cup type wind sensor was invented by Robinson in the 19th century. When the cups are rotated by the wind force, the rotation will generate a signal proportional to the speed. This signal can be fed to display and other devices. Old time cup type wind sensors were with four cups but now improved aerodynamics and for better results three cup wind sensors are common.

21. What is the working principle of wind sonic or ultrasonic wind sensor?

    Ultrasonic or ultrasound type of anemometers were developed in the 1950s. These make use of sound waves which are called ultrasound or ultra-sonic. Ultrasonic sound waves are generated and made to travel using four transducers. The time of flight principle is used to calculate the speed and direction of the wind.

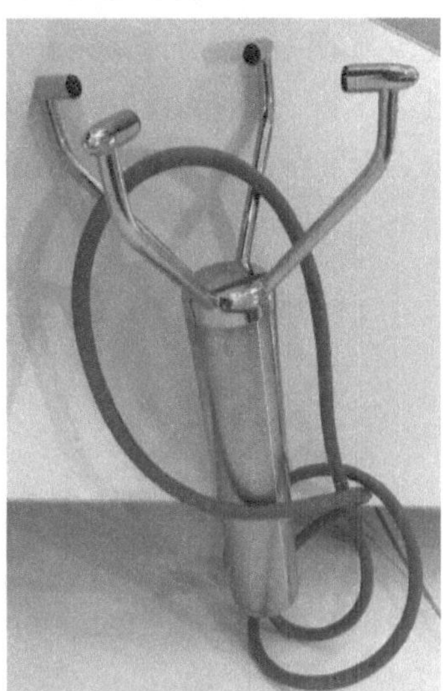

Fig: 9.9   Wind Sonic Wind Sensor

22. What is the working principle of Acoustic Resonance anemometers?

Acoustic resonance anemometers are relatively new equipment. These were invented in the year 1999 and patented by Savvas Kapartis. As compared to conventional sonic anemometers which measure based on how much time the sound waves take, these acoustic devices measure the speed and the direction of wind accurately. As the distance between the two sensors is fixed and so is the speed of sound in air. The time taken will vary depending upon the speed of prevalent wind and its direction.

23. What is the meaning and significance of "Wind Sensor Rejected" alarm?

    When the difference between the value measured by a sensor and previous values received exceeds cross a set limit. This will lead to rejection of the wind sensor. A wind sensor may also be rejected if the increase in wind speed/direction is more than a set limit on the DP system. Wind data will be frozen and wind model will be erroneous.

24. After wind sensor is rejected, what is proposed corrective measure?

    The first step should be to disable failed sensor. After carrying out checks of the wind sensor, check input interface to the DP controller. A rejected sensor may be accepted again either by deselecting and selecting again or by putting the DP system to standby mode and resetting it. If it is deselected and then selected again or if the DP system is set to Standby mode.

25. What is wind difference alarm when two wind sensors are used?

    If the difference in speed between two of the wind sensors is more than 6 m/s or difference in direction is more than 45.8°. Now the DPO must decide which is the good wind sensor and deselect/disable the one which is faulty.

26. What input is required to enable auto-heading control while in Joystick mode?

    It is the gyro which measures the heading of the vessel and rate of turn. To control the heading automatically, at least one gyro is required to be online.

27. What happens if all MRU/VRS's fail?

In case of failure of MRU/VRU, the position reference system input will not be compensated for roll and pitch.

28. Which movement does the Gyro Compass monitor?

Yaw movement of the vessel is being measured by gyro compass. This enables the vessels to measure heading of the ship and the rate of turn.

29. A DP Class 1 Vessel is fitted with two gyros. The gyros are observed to have a steady difference of 3 degrees. What is the recommended action?

The DPO must first observe both the gyros, specially the one which seems to be having difference. Compare them with the magnetic compass, apply offset correction to the one which is out and may continue operations. This gyro with an offset must be observed carefully.

30. While the vessel is working very close to a platform and the wind sensors are being blocked by the top structure. What action the DPO should initiate?

It is advised that when the vessels wind sensors are being blocked, the wind sensors cannot measure the correct wind and hence the wind model is spoiled. To avoid this, it is recommended to deselect the wind sensors.

CHAPTER 10
POSITION REFERENCE SENSORS (PRS)/ POSITION MEASURING EQUIPMENT (PME)

1. **What is PRS/PME?**

    Position Reference System or Position Measuring equipment are also called as PRS/PME. There are many types of PRS/ PME in use for the purpose of dynamic positioning. These work on different working principles and are used for different conditions and locations.

2. **What is a local, or relative positioning reference system?**

    A "Local" or "Relative" position reference sensor provides position locally and the position measured is relative to a known target fixed or moving. Examples of relative PRS – All Laser based PRS are in the category of local/relative PRS.

3. **Which reference system is used as a reference origin?**

    The reference sensor which is enabled first in the DP system and is accepted, will become the Reference origin. This reference system continues to be the reference for the other reference sensors, till it is changed. To change the reference origin, all online PRS must be deselected and now select the refence sensor which is required to be made the reference origin. In the figure below, GPS1 is indicated as the reference origin.

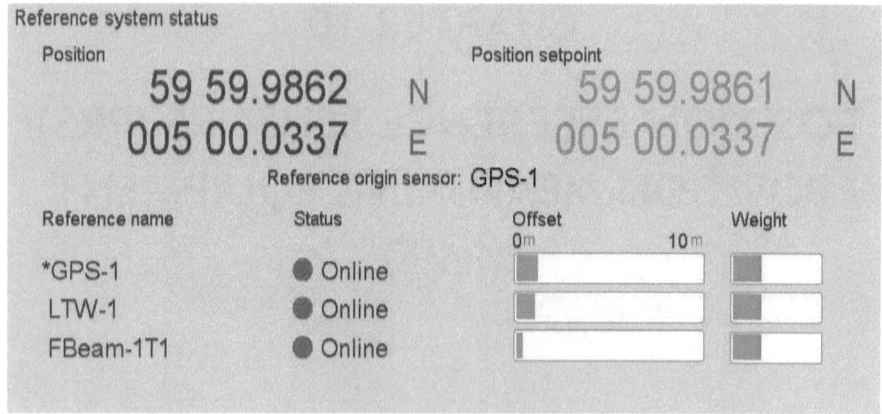

Fig: 10.1 Reference Origin (Courtesy Kongsberg)

4. What is an "absolute" position reference system?

An absolute position reference system measures the position in absolute terms. For an example the position measured by the GPS/DGPS is absolute.

5. What is HPR/HiPAP? What is it used for?

HPR stands for Hydroacoustic position reference and HiPAP stands for High Precision Acoustic positioning. These are the parts of the acoustic based position reference sensors. A sound wave travelling in water measures the position of the ship from a point of reference which either placed on the subsea surface or on a moving target like a remotely operated vehicle (ROV).

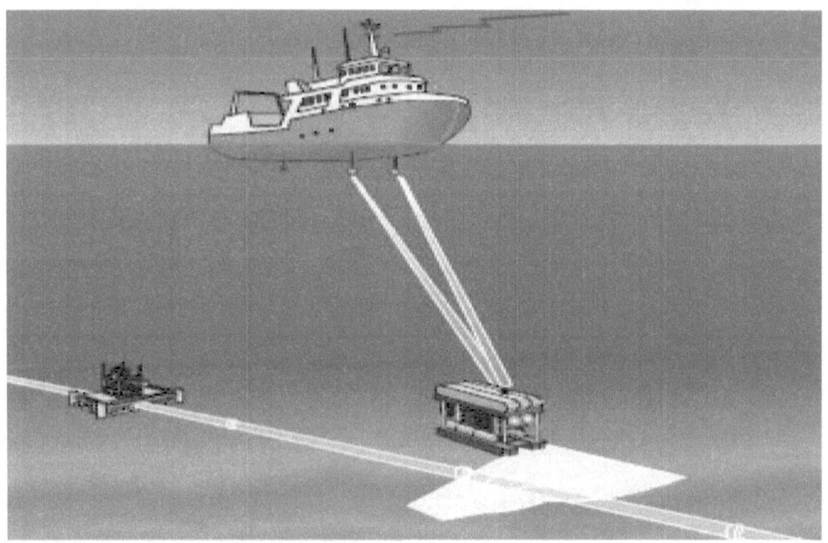

Fig: 10.2   HPR/HiPap System (Courtesy Kongsberg)

6. What is the purpose of the position reference sensors or position reference systems (PRS)?

    The PRS are used for measuring the surge and the sway movement of the vessel. Both these movements are on the horizontal plane. After measuring these movements arrangements are made to control these two movements along with the third movement i.e. yaw of the vessel by using the active thrust.

7. What are the main limitations on the use of Tautwire system?

    Tautwire system is probably the best position reference sensor onboard. However, this sensor also has certain limitations. While working in deep waters the sensor may have problems and when the Tautwire angle increases more than certain given limits, it may not give the desired results. So, the main problems while using a Tautwire system are angle of the wire and the water depth.

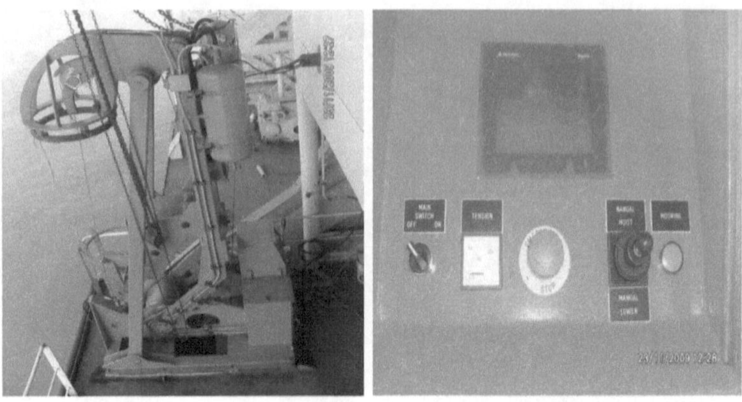

Fig: 10.3   Tautwire System (Courtesy Bandak Tautwire)

8.   What is the main problem with an inertial navigation system?

The position calculated drifts over time and needs to be corrected by another position reference system.

9.   What is Median Check?

This test is included in the DP control system to prevent a position reference system from causing a loss of position. The test is designed when three or more reference sensors are enabled. The figure below depicts median test on with the median circle set by the DP system.

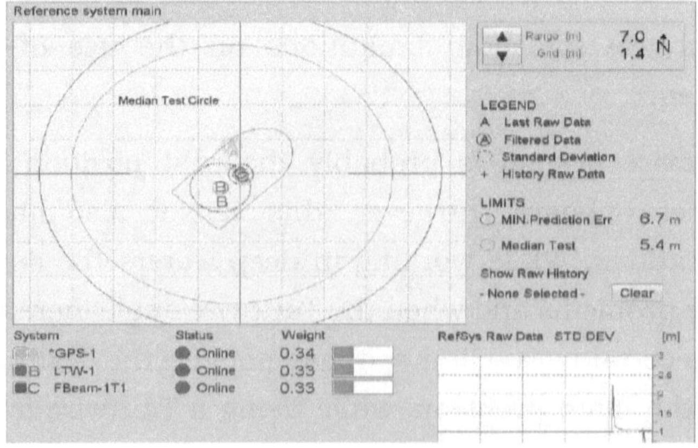

Fig: 10. 4   Median Test Circle (Courtesy Kongsberg)

10. What is "Differential" in DGPS?

    Differential is the difference between the measured (observed) position (raw observations) and a "known" or "Real" location. The Differential corrections are applied ashore and then transmitted to the ships.

11. What is DOP with reference to DGPS?

    DOP or Dilution of Precision is a measure of positioning quality.

12. What is NMEA or NMEA 0183?

    NMEA or National Marine Electronics Association format 1083 defines the various internal message formats transmitted to the DP system. Most sensors and PRS use this format. The figure below shows a NMEA string of DGPS.

Fig: 10.5   NMEA 0183 Sentence (GPS/DGPS Signal)

By looking at the signal (sentence) it may be inferred that the signal was received at 11 hrs, 35 minutes 29 seconds. 4205.037 is Northing reading, 1.07.09 is the Easting reading, 1 indicates GPS (2 indicates DGPS), 7 is the number of satellites available, 0.9 is the value of HDOP (horizontal dilution of precision), 54.8 is the height of antenna above main sea level, 43.6 Meters is Height of geoid (mean sea level) using WGS84, after this the empty field indicate time in seconds the update of DGPS (As shown in this signal it is indicated 1 means it is GPS(Differential corrections are failed) so the field is empty, the last digit 48 is preceded by an asterisk mark which denotes the Checksum data and end of the signal.

13. What is scintillation?

    Scintillation is the result of sunspots. This changes to radio waves caused by their interaction with the electron content of the ionosphere, released by the ionisation due to the heat of the radiated energy of the Sun, thereby causing poor reception.

14. What is Trilateration or Triangulation in GPS?

    Trilateration or triangulation requires three satellites to calculate a 3-dimensional location on the surface of the earth. Position can be measured after trilateration is complete, but the position may jump. To avoid this jump, a 4th satellite is used to remove the ambiguity from one of the two three-dimensional intersections. Hence the minimum number of satellites used for GPS system is four.

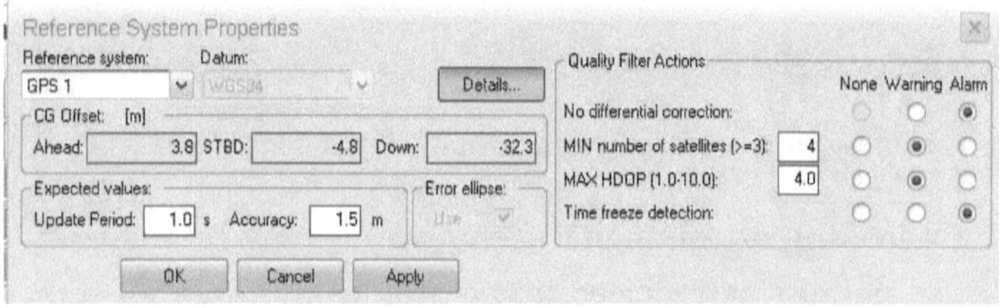

Fig: 10.6 Minimum Number of Satellites for GPS

15. What is ephemeral data or ephemeris?

    Ephemeris or ephemeral data may be defined as the complete information or the orbital data which the GPS may use to calculate the position by knowing the position of the satellites. Each satellite transmits has its own unique ephemeral data.

16. What is DGNSS?

    Differential GNSS (DGNSS) or Differential Global navigational Satellite system is the process wherein data is provided from a series of reference stations also known as base stations. These stations have a known and fixed position and they receive and process ephemeris data. The corrected data is then sent to the users which then be used correct their pseudo-ranges.

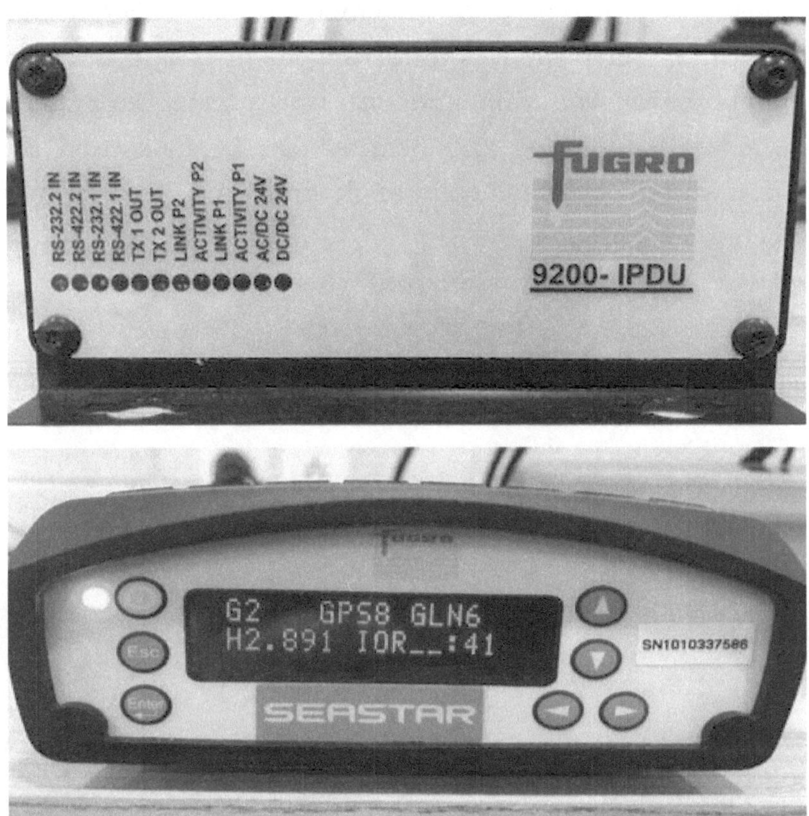

Fig: 10.7 Differential Global navigational Satellite system (DGNSS) (Courtesy Fugro)

17. Explain HDOP.

HDOP stands for horizontal dilution of precision and this term is used in satellite communication. Geometry and trigonometry are used to calculate the position of the satellites and its effects on the measurement. These values are expressed as a number. If the numbers are lower, it is considered better.

18. **Explain what is USBL or SSBL?**

Ultra-short baseline or some time also called super short baseline, is a type of arrangement for the HPR/HiPAP. In USBL or SSBL there is an arrangement of one transducer installed on the ship and one transponder launched on the seabed. Range and bearing can be measured using this system by measuring angle and time of travel by the acoustic signal.

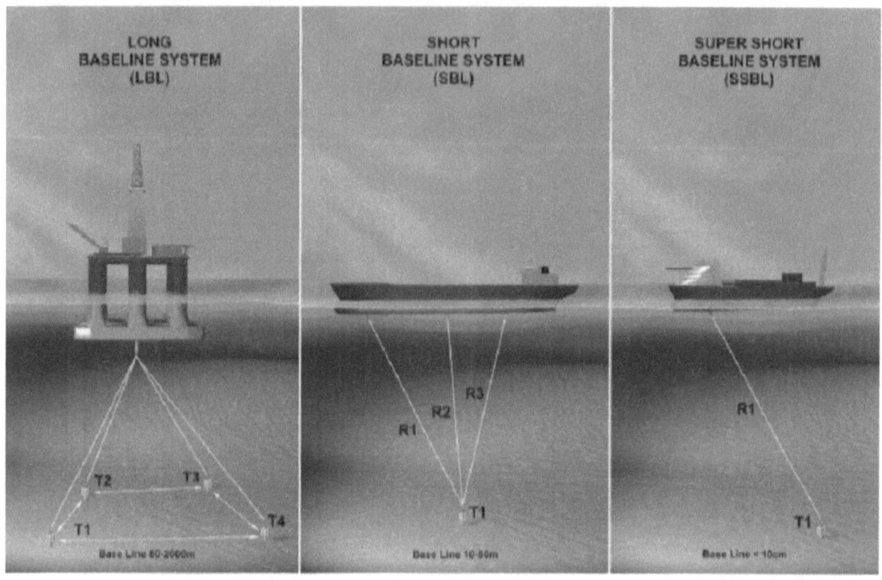

Fig 10.8 SSBL/SBL/LBL System (Courtesy Kongsberg)

19. **What is DQI in DGPS?**

It stands for Differential Quality Indicator. DQI indicates the quality of the position. If the quality of the position shown is less than 5, the colour background of the bar showing it will change to yellow. If it is going less than 2, the colour will change to red.

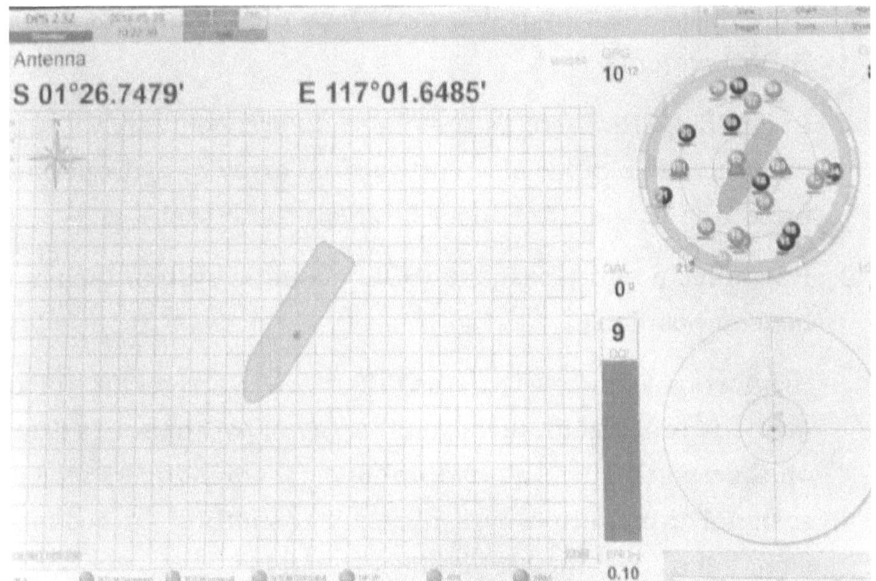

Fig: 10.9   Differential Quality Indicator (DQI) (Courtesy Kongsberg)

The DQI shown in the above figure is 9, which is very good. The estimate of position error (EPE) show is 0.10 meter, which indicates a very high level of accuracy.

20. Name the various factor that influence working of Hydro Acoustics.

   a) Noise generated from the ship's thrusters, other ships, drilling equipment, waves, other hydro acoustic activities nearby.

   b) Reflection of sound waves from the sea bottom, ship surface and other subsea structures.

   c) The Sound wave bending due to different temperature layers and the salinity of water.

   d) Loses due to Transmission as the waves undergo spreading and absorption

21. **How does SSBL or USBL measures the position in HPR/ HiPAP system?**

    In SSBL/USBL systems the phase difference in arrival time of an acoustic pulse at an orthogonal array of hydrophones fitted in a single transducer fitted on the vessel.

22. **How does a short baseline (SBL) acoustic system measure beacon position?**

    In short base line system, the difference in arrival time of an acoustic pulse at an orthogonal array of hydrophones fitted on the vessel. These all hydrophones or transducers receive a signal transmitted by a pinger transmitting an acoustic signal at a fixed interval and set frequency.

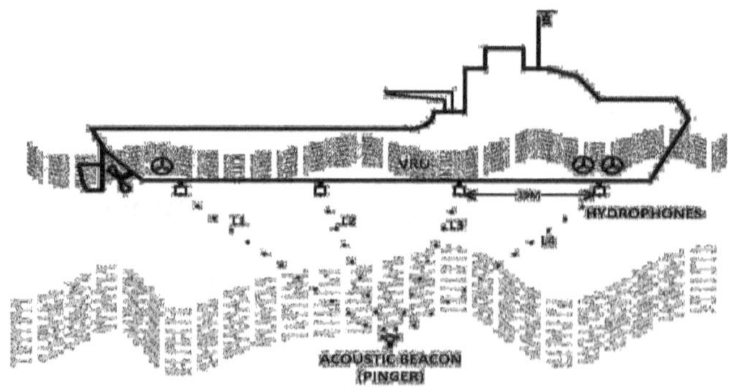

Fig: 10.10   Short Base Line System

23. **What activity on an 11 years cycle affects GPS and over what area of the globe?**

    Sunspots affecting areas near the magnetic equator that happens to run through most of the key deep-water oil exploration areas - Brazil, West Africa and the Far East. Sunspot activities results in GPS signal being adversely affected by the electromagnetic field created by the heat waves as during the 11 year cycle the earth is nearest to the sun.

24. What does DARPs stand for? Where do we use this equipment?

Differential Absolute and Relative Positioning System is consisting of DGPS and a UHF link on both the vessels. DARPS is used by shuttle tankers and FPSO to know where they are both in absolute position and relative to the FPSO's position.

25. What is an Artemis system? Where do we use Artemis?

Artemis is a microwave system (3Cm radar). This measures the range and bearing to the fixed or target unit, usually a FPSO with the shuttle tanker. Two identical units are used on both the vessels.

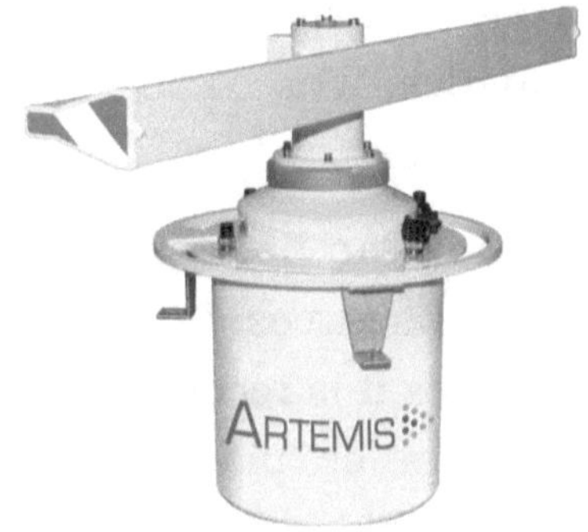

Fig 10.11   Artemis (Courtesy Guidance Navigation- Wartsila)

26. What is HDOP?

HDOP stands for horizontal dilution of position and is a function of the distribution of satellites in the sky for the GPS/DGPS functioning. Best HDOP values can be obtained if the satellites are evenly distributed/located in all four directions and appropriate elevation angle.

27. What is PDOP?

PDOP stands for precision dilution of position. Like HDOP, PDOP is also a function of the distribution of satellites in the sky for the GPS/DGPS functioning. Best PDOP values, similar to HDOP values can be obtained if the satellites are evenly distributed/located in all four directions and appropriate elevation angle.

28. As per requirements, a DP class 2 or 3 vessel is fitted with four PRS. These include, two DGNSS, one Taut wire and one Laser sensor each. In this case, why is it advisable that the DPO should prefer to count two DGNSS as one PRS?

    Redundancy is very important aspect of a DP2/3 vessel. In case of DGNSS, a common mode of failure will render both DGNSS useless for DP applications hence it is recommended that that the DPO must consider both DGNSS as one PRS.

29. Placement of HPR transponders at the seabed is very important in acoustics. What is the best placement of HPR transponder should be?

    The acoustic systems can be easily disturbed by the noise generated by various sources. To avoid the noise from the thrusters/wind/waves it is recommended that the acoustic beacons/transponders be placed down wind and down current as far as possible.

30. While using DGPS, what is the minimum number of satellites required for good position fixing?

    Trilateration can find out position with the help of three satellites but for a good position fixing four satellites are required.

31. List the positioning reference systems (PRS) that can use multiple targets are:

    The Laser based PRS (Fanbeam. Cyscan and Spot Track) and Frequency Modulated Continuous Wave Radars (FMCW Radars i.e. Radius and Radascan) can use multiple targets.

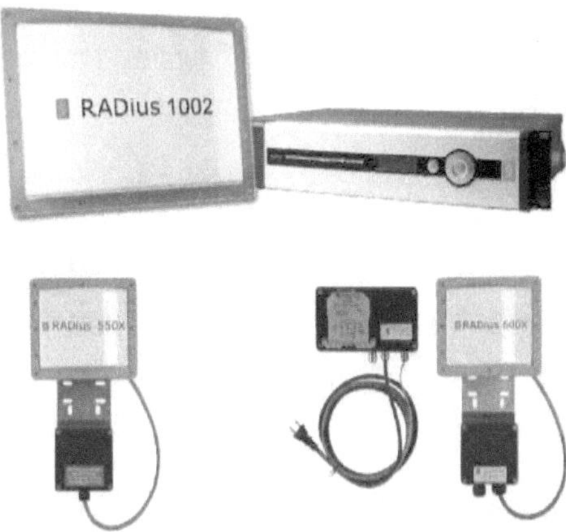

Fig: 10.12   FMCW Radius (Courtesy Kongsberg)

Fig: 10.13   FMCW Radascan (Courtesy Guidance Marine-Wartsila)

32. When using a Taut Wire positioning system what happens when the vessel is working in very deep waters?

   While working in deep waters and using Tautwire system, the accuracy of the PRS may deteriorate. The accuracy will also go down while the angle of the wire increases beyond certain limits.

33. What is a freeze test on PRS?

   A freeze test on PRS is carried out by the DP computer to assess if the signals received are frozen. If it is observed that the variation in the measured position is less than a system set limit over a given period of time, the position-reference system may be rejected.

34. What is prediction test on PRS?

A Prediction test detects sudden jumps in the measurement of PRS position or large systematic deviations in the measured position. The prediction test will remove statistically wrong measurements.

35. What is median test on PRS?

A median test, as the name suggests middle value, is designed to detects position measurements that differ from the median position value. If the value is more than a predefined limit, a message is generated. Median test is mainly designed to detect slowly drifting position-reference systems.

36. What is the speed of sound signal in sea water?

The sound travels at a speed of 1500m per second in sea water.

37. What is the speed of a sound signal in air?

At 20 °C (68 °F), a sound signals will travel at the speed of about 343 metres per second.

38. What is approximately the speed of sound in vacuum?

Sound is form of energy... requires a media to travel, vacuum provides no media and hence sound cannot travel in vacuum.

39. If a vessel is fitted with two taut wires, can two taut wires be counted as two independent PRS?

Yes, two taut wires may be counted as two independent PRS provided if they are supplied with independent, main power supply, UPS supply, compressed air, cooling etc. The purpose is to avoid common mode of failure.

40. What are the main limitations of a taut wire as PRS?

    The main limitations are as below:

    - May damage subsea equipment

    - Difficulties is deployment and recovery in heavy weather

    - Limitations on range and angle

    - Limitations to water depth @300-350 meters

    - Wire rope care and hindrances

41. What are the main advantages of a TW as position reference system?

    - Simple technology

    - Mechanical movement measures angle

    - Angle then converted to distance moved

    - DPO can easily verify angle for confirmation

    - No signal interference

42. Under what conditions can a 'relative' position reference system be considered as an 'absolute' position reference system?

    A relative PRS may be considered as an absolute PRS only if its target is installed/fixed on a nonmoving platform or a moored or DP vessel.

43. The frequencies used by acoustic systems (HPR & HIPAP) in DP is generally in the range of 20kHz to 30kHz. Why this range of frequency has been chosen?

This a range of frequency is chosen for the simple reason that in this band of frequency the thruster noise interference is minimum.

44. Do the PRS/PME get affected by vessel roll and pitch?

Yes, the performance of the PRS/PME is badly affected by the vertical axis movements of the vessel i.e.in particularly the roll and the pitch... The most affected are the ones which are fitted further away from the CG, as the movement is maximum. The roll and pitch movements are hence measured and compensated for/offset for the roll and pitch movements.

45. What settings/arrangements can be done to protect position jump while using two DGNSS and some satellites are jumping (Coming in & out). Both DGNSS are using the same constellation.

It is recommended that both DGNSS utilise different elevation masks. This will warn the operator and give some time as when a satellite is going out and coming in and only one DGNSS will be affected at one time due to different elevation masking.

46. In acoustics, using a super short base line (SSBL) or ultra-short base line (USBL) system how is position of a transponder calculated?

The position of transponder in SSBL/USBL system is calculated by knowing the phase difference of the acoustic signals received in different elements of a single transducer unit. The figure below shows the working principle of a SSBL/USBL system.

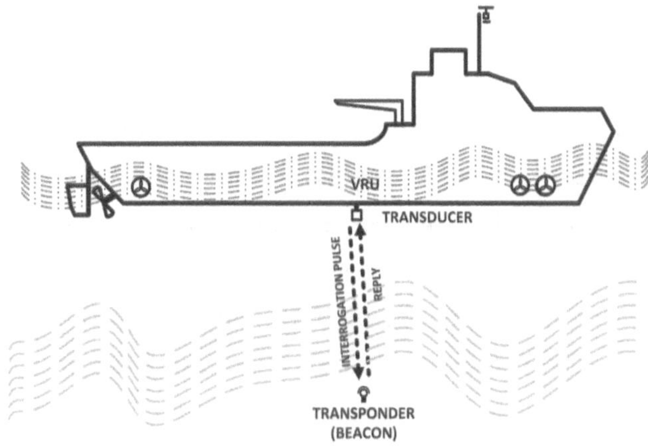

Fig. 10.14   SSBL/USBL

47. In hydro acoustic system using long base line system, (LBL) how is the vessel position measured?

While using long base line (LBL), the vessel position is measured by measuring the range between single transducer installed on the vessel and the calibrated array of transponders installed on the seabed. A sketch of a long base line system is depicted below.

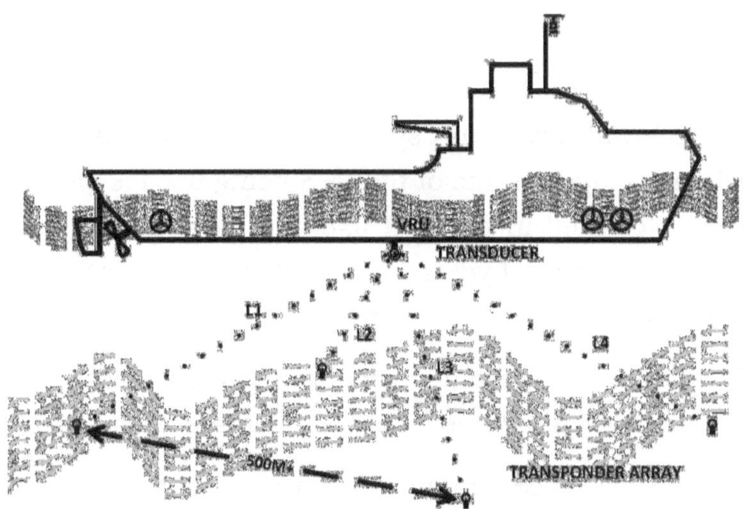

Fig: 10.15   Long Base Line

48. Explain the operating principle of a responder and transponder.

    A transponder is designed to respond when acoustic interrogation pulse is received. Both the interrogation and reply are sent through water using acoustic pulse. Whereas in a responder, interrogation pulse is received by the responder fitted on top of ROV via the umbilical cord. The response from the responder is transmitted through water. This helps in avoiding the noise problems one way.

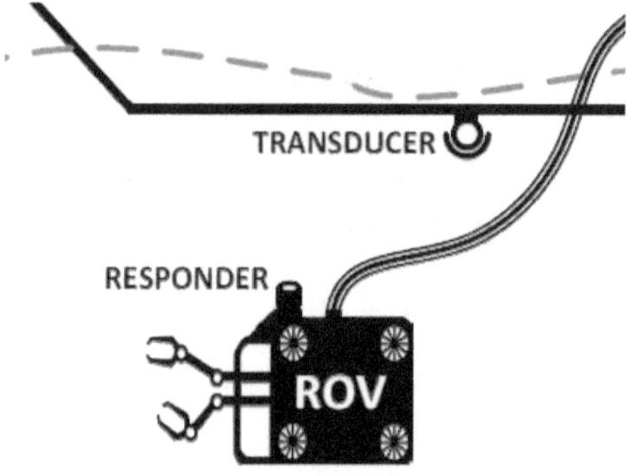

Fig: 10.16   Responder (Used on ROV)

49. Explain the principle of operation of an inertial navigation system INS or Hydroacoustic Aided INS or HAINS.?

    The inertial navigation system (INS) provides position data when the update rate of the PRS being used is slow. For an example to fill in position fixes for slow update rate deep water acoustics hydroacoustic inertial navigation system (HAINS) is used.

50. How does an inertial navigation system measure input? With those input/s how does it calculate position?

    It measures acceleration. Acceleration is then integrated to arrive at the velocity. Velocity is now further integrated to arrive at the position of the vessel.

51. It is commonly observed that the inertial navigation system drifts. What are the reasons for thus drift?

    Acceleration is particularly important input for INS. Any error in measuring acceleration may result in an increasing error as acceleration is integrated over the time to measure the position.

52. Which are two generally used methods for use of inertial navigation in dynamic positioning?

    For using INS into DP there are two methods.

    - Loosely coupled INS and

    - Tightly coupled INS

53. Why there is need for the position reference sensors (PRS) or position measuring equipment (PME)?

    PRS/PME inputs are required before surge or sway can be automatically controlled. Hence for auto position mode it is must to have an active PRS.

54. How does the GPS determine vessel position?

    The GPS receiver acquires radio signals from available satellites. These signals received help in measuring time of signal reception. As the satellite/s position is known, this helps in determining multiple ranges for each satellite. Minimum three satellites are required but, a fourth satellite helps in finding the accurate position.

55. The accuracy and reliability of which position reference system can be improved by utilising a HAIN system (HAINS)?

    Hydro Acoustic Aided Navigation System (HAINS) is used to increase the accuracy of Riser Angle System. This mainly used for drill ships.

56. How the differential corrections for GNSS systems may be transmitted by the shore-based stations?

    The shore-based stations may use MF/HF transmission depending upon the distance of the receiving vessel. If the vessel location far from the shore-based station, the satellites are used to transmit the differentially corrected signals.

57. What is sunspot activity?

    Reception of GPS satellite data is affected by ionization due to the radiated heat from sun. This ionization will hamper the GPS signal reception.

58. A vessel is operating near a rig on DP. Suddenly there is a change in weather and heavy thunders are experienced. Which position reference sensor will be affected by this heavy thunder?

    Hydro-acoustic systems (HPR & HiPAP) range measurements can be affected by heavy thunders as the equipment works on the principle of sound travelling in water.

59. A DP vessel is working close to a structure (approximately 100 meters). Due to change in climatic conditions, thick fog is prevalent now. Which reference sensor/s would you recommend not using under these situations?

    In fog conditions, it is not recommended to use laser-based sensors as the performance of such PRS may be unreliable.

60. Name the activities/factors which can adversely affect DGNSS positioning reference systems.

    The onboard DGNSS will be affected by certain microwave-based communication/activities from the close surrounding. Sunspot activity will also hamper the reception of DGNSS and high HDOP values may result in poor performances.

61. What is best scenario to use Tautwire system as one of the PRS in DP.

A Tautwire may be used as one of the PRS when the vessel is operating in 70 to 300 metre water depths. The performance of the Tautwire in these water depths is the best.

62. With reference to Hydroacoustic Position Reference (HPR) System, define a Responder Beacon.

A responder is an underwater device fitted on ROV. It gets the interrogation pulse from the HPR system via the umbilical cord and sends the reply pulse though water. This way the disturbances in communication are reduced one way at least.

63. Name the most commonly used position sensors (PRS) on board DP enabled vessels?

The following are the commonly used PRS onboard the DP enabled vessels. For easy understanding these may be catagoriesd in two i.e. Absolute and Relative PRS.

Absolute PRS: In the absolute category the GPS or DGPS, Tautwire system and hydro-Acoustic system are included. The hydroacoustic may be further divided into three type namely long base line (LBL), short base line (SBL) and ultra-short base line system (USBL).

Relative PRS: The relative category of PRS include laser-based system which include Cyscan, Fanbeam and Spot track. The Artemis and the new types of radars i.e. based on frequency modulated continuous wave radars i.e. RADius and RADascan are also included in the relative category of PRS.

64. A vessel on DP working with two identical DGPS and one Fanbeam system. Considering equal spread of fixes, what will be the weightages for these PRSs?

As per the statement, all the PRS will have equal weightage as the spread of the fixes from the PRSs indicate that that their accuracy is the same. They may share weightage of @33% each. However, in case of the circumstances that the GPS satellites are blocked and thus lowering the accuracy of both the DGPSs, the Fanbeam system will increase in its weightage.

65. Name four of the most utilized position reference sensors (PRS) in the offshore DP market.

The four most used DP sensors which are used to measure the vessels position for DP operations are as below. The order doesn't define their importance.

- DGPS

- Laser based sensors (Fanbeam, Cyscan, Spot track)

- FMCW (RADius and RADascan)

- Hydro-Acoustic (HPR and Hipap)

66. Name two errors on DGPS which cannot be corrected?

Multipath error and the signal noise errors cannot be corrected during the differential correction process in the shore-based stations.

67. How do we verify the stability and heading accuracy of the Laser based position reference system?

Select single reflector and rotate the vessel heading @15 degrees both sides. Observe the position and heading after the vessel is stabilized after each move. The heading should be within 2 degrees and position should not go more than 2 meters overshoot.

68. How is DGPS failure tested?

DGPS failure may be tested by disconnecting the serial input line. After identifying the signal cable, disconnect one of the two connections and observe the GPS telegram timeout alarm. This will also be followed by more GPS related alarms including differential and weightages etc.

69. How is Cyscan heading test carried out?

This test may require activating Cyscan as the only PRS. Rotate the ships heading to port and starboard. The position is expected to be stabilized within a few meters and heading overshoot may not be more than 2 degrees.

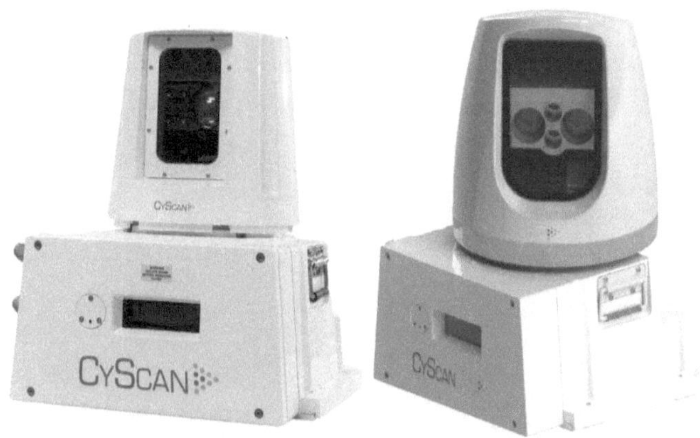

Cyscan Mk 4 & Cyscan AS

Fig: 10.17   CYSCAN (Courtesy Guidance Marine - Wartsila)

70. What is Cyscan failure test?

Like any other PRS failure test, identify the connections in the DP controller (Input output devices) and disconnect one of the serial input line connection. Cyscan degraded/ rejected/telegram timeout etc. may be observed.

CHAPTER 11
AUTOMATION AND NETWORKING IN DP SYSTEMS

1. **What is Wind Sensor Not Ready Alarm?**

When one of the enabled wind sensors has lost its OK/ Ready signal, wind sensor not ready alarm is activated. If this wind sensor was the one chosen as "Preference" one, the DP system automatically will change over to the next wind sensor. Most of the wind sensors have their own BITE (Built in Test Equipment) to generate this alarm. The DPO must enable the other available sensor.

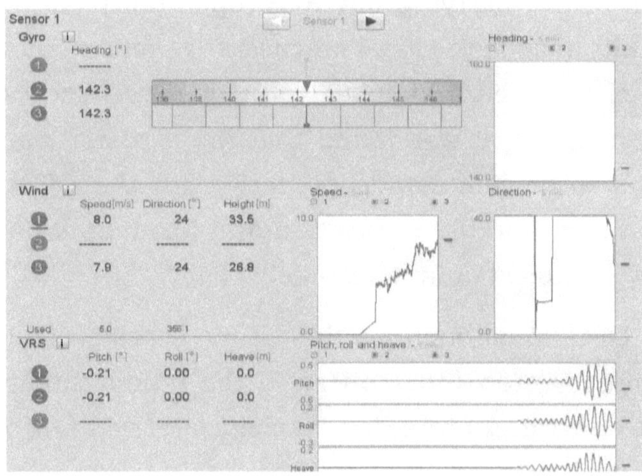

Fig: 11.1   Wind Sensor # 1 Not Ready Alarm (Courtesy Kongsberg)

2. What is a data timeout?

Data communication between various equipment including sensors, power, thruster and other special devices is ensured with a time frame, If the data fails to arrive within the expected time frame, it timed out and warning/alarm is generated. The figure below shows the data time out alarm for the transponder 1 and transponder 2 of Radius. Followed by these alarms is the Radius No Reply/Rejected Alarm.

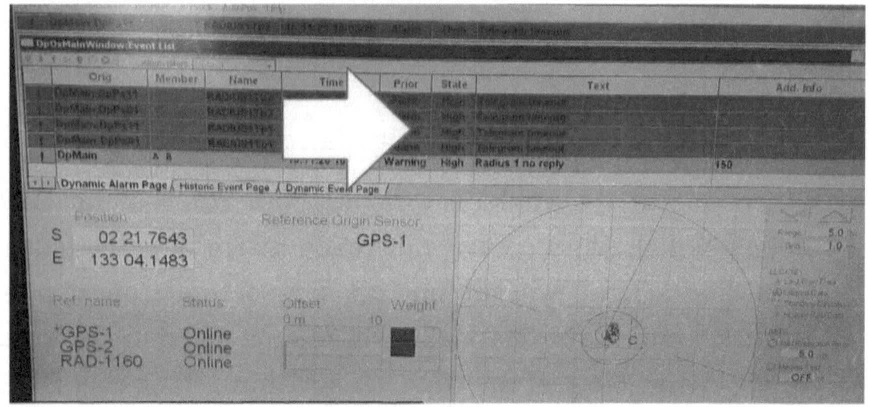

Fig: 11.2 Data Timeout (Courtesy Kongsberg)

3. A DP vessel carrying out ROV operations close to a rig. A faulty feedback signal warned that one of the two bow tunnel thrusters has failed to full force. On inspection by the engineers, it was found that the thruster running and seems to be functioning properly. But the DPO confirms that there is a loss of position and heading. What is most appropriate action at this time?

The DPO must identify the faulty thruster and activate emergency stop the soonest. If the faulty thruster is not shut down in a few seconds, the vessel will not be able to hold position.

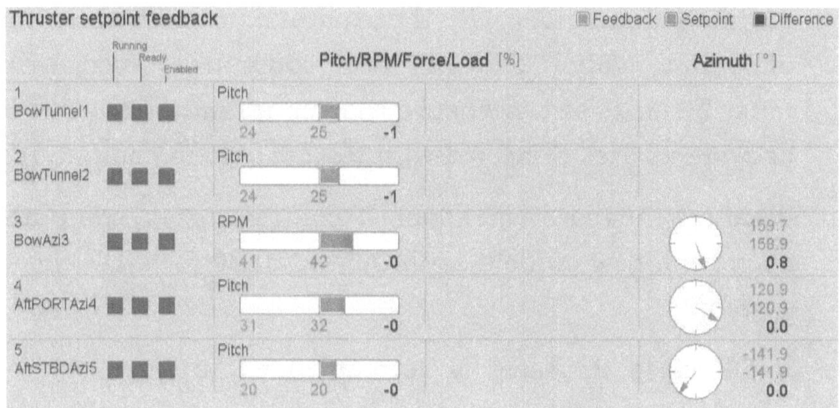

Fig: 11.3   Thruster Command/Setpoint and Feedback Signals (Courtesy Kongsberg)

4. What are new requirements for automatic transfer of control for DP computers as per new guidelines IMO/MSC 1580?

    IMO/MSC 1580 recommends that the computers in DP systems should be arranged in such a way that redundancy is ensured by automatic changeover. The changeover should be smooth and quick after detection of failure of the online computer. The changeover must not affect the position or heading of the vessel.

5. With the new IMO guidelines (1580) what arrangements have been made to ensure integrity and isolation of DP computer?

    A New section emphasising the required isolation and integrity of DP systems has been added to take care of the isolation and integration.

    As per the new guidelines, it is recommended to have a good isolation between the DP computers and the other onboard computers so that the integrity of the DP computers is ensured. Both methods of hardware and software isolation may be utilized along with the separation of cables and lines of communication between these computers. Special care must be exercised to ensure that no unauthorized devices or systems are connected with the DP system computers.

6. What are the requirements of DP control system/computers as per the new guidelines IMO/MSC 1580 for a DP class 2 system?

    A DP class 2 vessel is recommended to have at least two computers so that in case of failure of one the other computer can be used. This should result in an automatic changeover and thereby maintaining the vessels position keeping capability. The redundancy arrangement is created in such a way that any changes due to data transfer, various interfaces, facilities of alignment and routine self-checking must not result into failure of both the computers. If any of the computer fails, or the other computer not ready to accept or take over the controls, an alarm is generated.

7. What are new requirements as per IMO/MSC 1580 regarding the DP operator station (DP Control Station)?

    As per the new guidelines highlighted in the IMO/MSC letter 1580, it is recommended to install the DP control station in such a place that the operator has a good view of the vessel surroundings. The following DP equipment are recommended but not limited to be fitted on the control station of the DP system.

    *   DP operator station with joystick control and an independent joystick control which is also known as CJOY or compact joystick.

    *   Thruster control levers to control the thruster manually.

- System to change over the different modes of DP

- Emergency stops for the thrusters

- Communication

- Position reference systems' Human Machine Interface when considered necessary.

8. What are the new requirements as per IMO/MSC 1580 for independent Joystick (IJS)?

Each DP system must have an independent joystick system. This is called independent as its not connected to the main DP controller. Some DP manufacturers also call it as compact joystick

In case of failure of main DP system, this independent joystick can be used to maneuver the vessel to safety using this system. IJS normally have an option of automatic heading control. Also, an alarm must warn the DP operator when IJS have a failure.

A

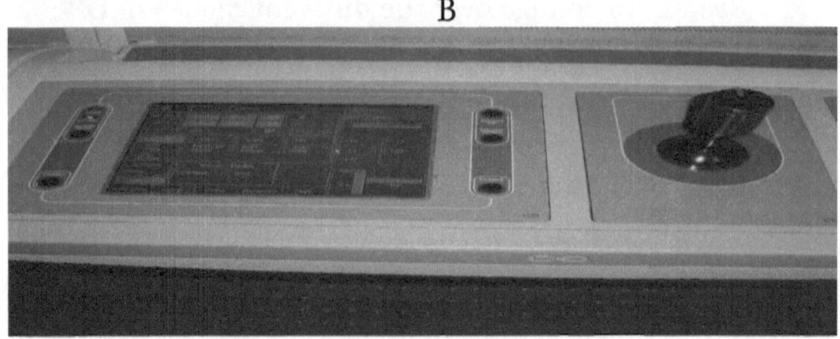

Fig: 11.4 Independent Joystick (IJS) – Courtesy (Kongsberg for A and Converteam for B)

9. What are the main requirements of DP control system for a class 2 DP system?

A DP class 2 system must be supported by a redundant control system. When there is a failure on one system, the other system must take over and should be able to continue holding vessels position and heading.

10. What are the requirements of DP control system for a DP 3 vessel?

The DP control system of a DP 3 vessel must have triple redundancy. One of the redundancies is provided in A/60 bulkhead separation. This control will be able to work and take control of the vessel and maintain her heading and position when the main system is failed due to fire or flooding.

11. What is the recommended arrangement for redundant computers for DP?

For redundancy and safety, the redundant computers must be arranged in such a way that automatic transfer of command is achieved. The changeover is designed to be bump less and there should be no loss of heading or position control when such changeovers take place.

12. What type of arrangement is available on DP control panel for various alarms and warning?

Whenever there is failure detected in the interfaced devices i.e. sensors, positions reference sensors, power, thruster and other special equipment, an alarm is expected to be initiated. This alarm must generate an audible and visual warning system to warn the DP operator and other DP professionals and locations. All such occurrences must be recorded/printed. Also, the DP system must be able to display to the DP professionals an explanation and details of such alarms with a possible way to handle to failed situation and its remedy. It is also important that the DP system control must be able to protect the fault being spread over to the pother redundant system.

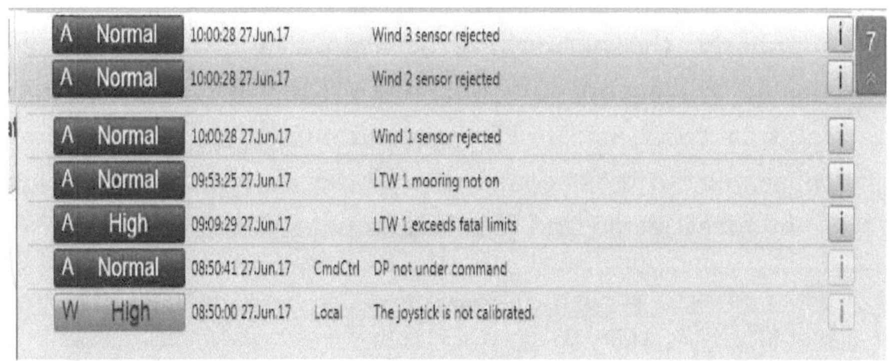

Fig: 11.5   Alarm View – Seven Alarm visible (Courtesy Kongsberg)

13. What is a general arrangement for networking between operator stations/workstations of DP system?

When there are more than one operator stations, these are connected by network. This networking of the stations is carried out using stand networking procedures and protocols. The figure below shows connectivity between OS1 and OS2.

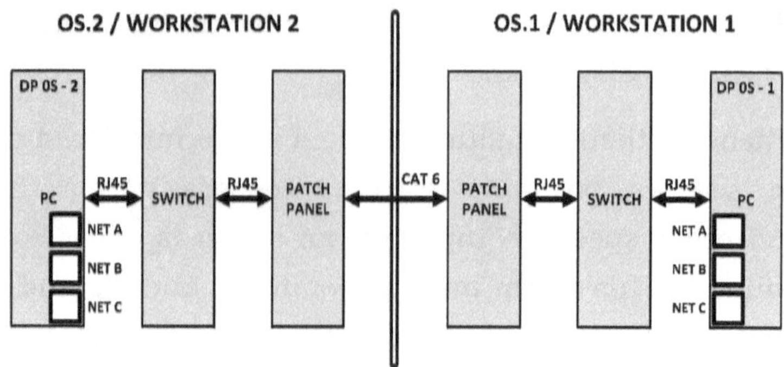

Fig: 11.6   Networking Between OS1 and OS 2

14. How is networking tested in a DP system?

The dual networking may be tested by unplugging the cable (Net A or Net B). Within some time observe Net A/B alarm "Error Net A" or Error Net B" accordingly. This may be followed by other alarms like process station (PS) degraded.

Similarly, the networking between two PS also may be tested by disconnecting one of the "REDNET" cables. Other alarms such as DP PS no communication may be now observed. In most common way the networking problems may investigated and checked by using "Ping Command".

Receiving Station	Sending Stat...	IpAddress	Msg pr.100 sec	Lost Msg
DP-OS3	DP-OS3	172.23.101.10	1	
DpPs01,DpPs0‹	Unknown	172.23.101.6	1	
	Unknown	172.23.101.3	1	
	Unknown	172.23.101.2	1	
	Unknown	172.23.101.1	1	
	Unknown	172.23.0.100	1	

Fig: 11.7   Networking (IP Address) – (Courtesy Kongsberg)

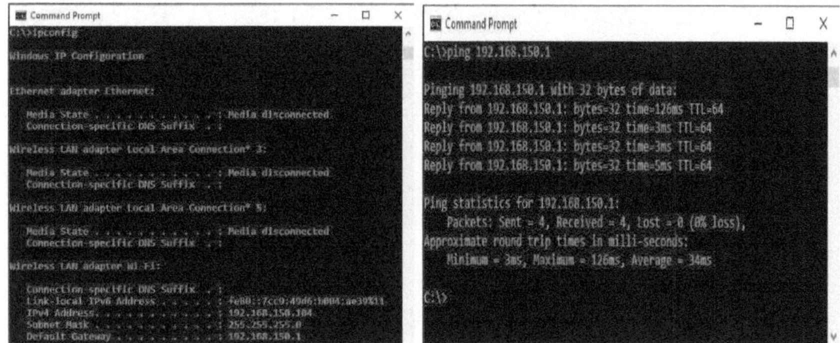

Fig: 11.8 Command Prompt

As shown above in the figure, the ping command sent four pings and each ping is responded with the time frame defined i.e. 3 milli seconds to 126 milli seconds. So, it confirms that the networking is healthy.

15. How do we test a networking cable (RJ45)?

RJ 45 cables are easily tested using cable tester. Other method of testing the same may not give results that can be depended on. By removing both ends of the cable and inserting the same into the two parts of the cable tester, the cable can be tested. If all the eight LEDs are working good, indicates that the connectivity id good. In some testers, the test is done by checking the pairs of connections (indicating four pairs).

Fig: 11.9 Network Cable Tester

The tester shown above has a pair of testers. Bothe ends of the cable can be inserted and RJ 45 cable can be tested very quickly and with confidence. Before using, it is good idea to check the battery of the tester.

CHAPTER 12

TEST AND TRIALS, CONSEQUENCE ANALYSIS, CAPABILITY PLOT, FOOTPRINT AND MOTION PREDICTION

1. Name the organizations which publish guidance on DP operations?

   Marine Technology Society of USA, (MTS DP Committee) and International marine Contractors Association UK (IMCA) are the main organizations who publish various guidelines.

2. What is considered as the 'three-legged stool' of Dynamic Positioning?

   The three-legged stools as usually called in DP circles is made up of design, people and operations. Operations are carried out by the well-trained people using a well designed and tested DP system.

3. What do the class DP notations rules deal with and what do they not deal with?

   The DP class notations, deal with required equipment which makes it easy to get a DP class. But the class notations do not deal with operations or the capability of the DP system.

4. Describe the four key parameters to be considered for any DP operation?

   The four key parameters are:

   • Time to terminate the operations (TTT),

   • Work area water depth,

   • Proximity to structures and

   • Simultaneous operations (SIMOPS).

5. What DP Vessels typically have a full traffic light system (Green/Yellow/Red) between the DP control position and the other positions that need to be informed so as to act on a change of status?

   The following vessels normally have a full traffic light system installed:

   • Mobile offshore drilling units generally referred to as MODU's,

   • Diving Support Vessels (DSVs)

   • Heavy Lift Crane Vessels

   • Cable/Pipe Laying Vessels

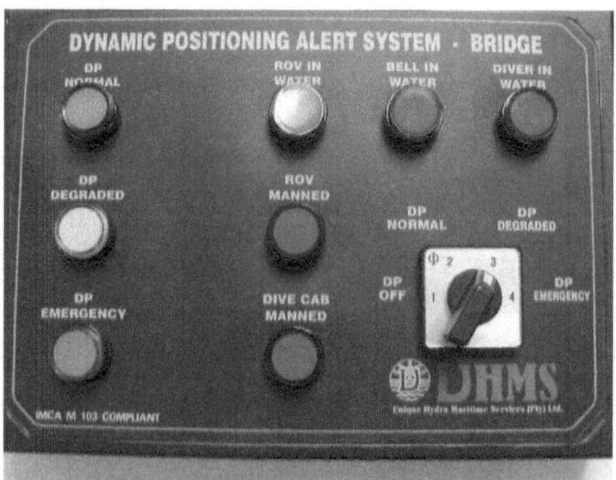

Fig: 12.1   Traffic Light/DP Alert System (Courtesy UHMS)

6. Name a few non offshore related vessels which are now being fitted with DP?

   Because of safety reason the Cruise liners and the Super Yachts are considering for DP.

7. Why is deployment of saturation diving has reduced than it used to be earlier?

   Due to technological advancements, the modern ROVs are much capable and reliable. These underwater robots can perform multitasking and therefore have reduced the use of saturation diving.

8. What is a hidden failure?

   A hidden failure may be defined as a dormant failure which is known only after the first failure occurs. A hidden failure may not be evident to the user or the operator unless another (resultant) failure makes it evident.

9. What is the method by which the station keeping capabilities of a DP vessel are depicted?

   It is the capability plot which shows the position keeping capabilities of a DP vessel.

10. How do you define a capability plot for a dynamically positioned vessel?

    Capability plot of a dynamically positioned vessel may be defined as a polar plot or may be a number of polar plots. These plots are sometimes referred to as envelopes. These envelops/plots show a DP vessel's theoretical capability in various environmental conditions, for different thruster and power generation combinations.

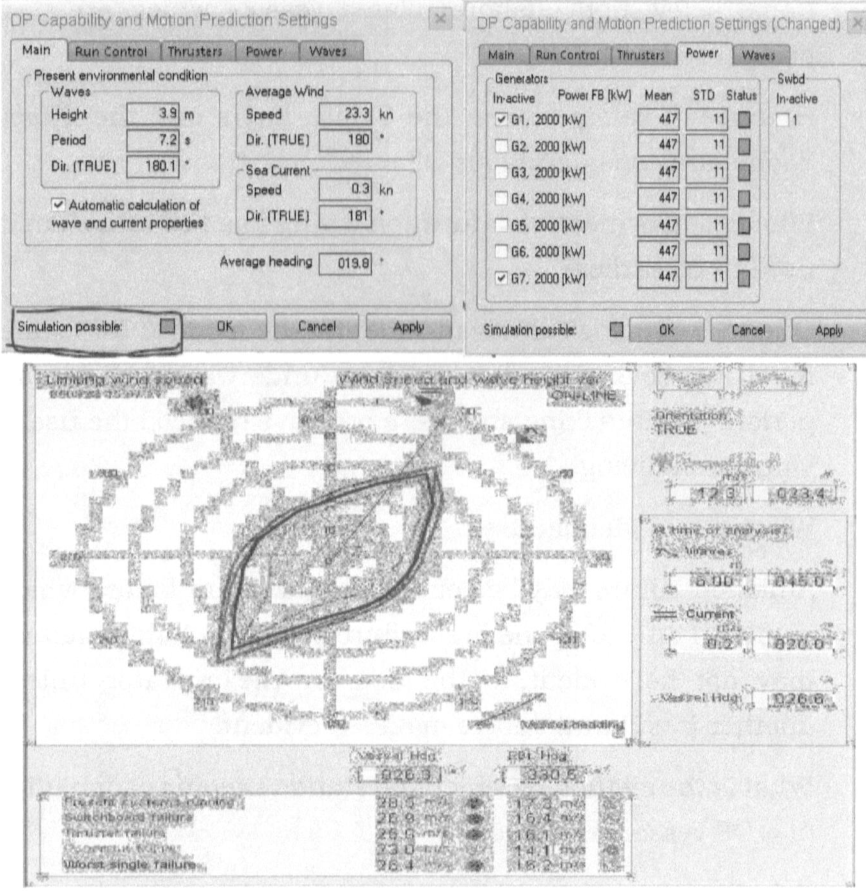

Fig: 12.2 Capability Plot (Courtesy Kongsberg)

11. What is the main guidance on how to produce capability plots for a DP vessel?

Specification for DP Capability Plots IMCA M 140 may be referred to for guidance. Also refer the standard operating procedures and the vessel specific DP operator manual.

12. What does a capability plot show?

A capability plot shows that under what kind of environmental conditions and using which thrusters/power a DP vessel can hold station.

13. What is the relation between the capability and operability of a DP vessel? Is capability and operability the same thing for a DP vessel??

    The capability and operability are not the same for any DP vessel. Operability is defined as the limits to which the operations may be carried out. But for safety reasons, operations may have to be abandoned before the capability limits are reached.

14. What is ERN? What is the significance for ERN?

    ERN stands for Environmental Regulatory Numbers. This notation is given by classification society DNV indicating the capability of the DP vessel. ERN is a theoretical calculation method developed in the 1970's by Mr. Holger Røkeberg of Det Norske Veritas. ERN may not be an absolute method for a DP vessel to calculate the station capability. Notwithstanding this fact, the ERN is considered a simple tool which helps in comparing the station keeping capability between various DP enabled vessels.

15. What is generally considered as a weakness of ERN when it just introduced?

    It was observed at that point of time that ERN does not consider worst case failure or limitations on power.

16. America Bureau of Shipping (ABS) also introduced a similar notation like ERN. What is this known as?

    The ABS introduced SKP, which stands for "Station Keeping Performance". SKP notation indicates that the station keeping performance of the DP enabled vessel has been verified using analysis for the designed environmental conditions. SKP has four categories (a, b, c, and d).

17. What is SKP (a,b,c,d) Notation form ABS?

    SKP (a, b, c, d): DP station keeping performance for a given environmental location.

    "a" defines the probability of a ship holding position when subjected to a set of environmental conditions and all thrusters operating.

    "b" Defines the probability that the ship can hold position when subjected to a particular conditions and environment with the defined worst-case failure (WCF) condition.

    "c" defines the Current speed in knots either owner specified, or standard used 1.5 kt.

    "d" Defines the environment location, which may be specified by owner or standard used is North Sea conditions.

18. What is EHS notation for ABS certified DP systems?

    Enhanced system notation (EHS), is provided as a supplement information for DPS-series notations certified by ABS. EHS recognizes that the system is over and above the general DPS notations. EHS applies to – Power Plant and Propulsion System of a ship and is represented by notation: (EHS-P). Control System enhancements are represented by: (EHS-C). Fire and Flood Protection System for s vessel may be represented by: (EHS-F) – A/60 bulkhead requirements.

19. What are the notations by Lloyds (LR) which can be compared to DNV's Environmental Regularity Numbers for rating DP vessels?

    Lloyds Performance Capability Rating commonly known as PCR are the notations for this purpose. In mid-eighties LR introduced Performance Capability Rating for DP vessels.

20. What are the PCR ratings by LR?

    - LR uses two numbers: (xx: yy).

    - XX is the % of time the vessel can keep position providing all systems are working.

    - YY is the % of time the vessel can keep position if the most effective thruster fails.

21. What are the components of the environment considered for the Capability plot a DP vessel?

    The components of environmental force considered while designing the capability plot are: Wind, waves and current. These are forces acting on to the ship.

22. What are the various criticality levels for DP vessel FMECA trails?

    Criticality – Levels used in DP operations are as below-

    - High,

    - Medium,

    - Low and

    - Very Low.

23. What is TAGOS?

    TAGOS stand for Thruster and Generator Operating Strategy. It's an operational document describing how generators and thruster of various sizes and capacities to run for that operation.

24. What is ASOG and WSOG?

    ASOG stands for Activity Specific Operational Guidelines and WSOG stands for Well Specific Operational Guidelines. Bothe are interchangeably used. When the activities are near a well ASOG is called WSOG. Every well may have its own WSOG.

25. What is CAM or CAMO?

CAMO stands for Critical Activity Mode of Operation. Both are used interchangeably. CAMO is used when a DP enabled vessel must stay on position after the worst-case failure has occurred.

26. What is TAM?

TAM is task Appropriate Mode. This mode us used when the DP enabled vessel may not be required to hold position after a worst-case failure has occurred. Example and comparison of TAM and CAM for a cable laying vessel. TAM may be used when the vessel is laying cable in open waters. CAM will use when the vessel is laying cable within 500 meters zone.

27. What may be prominent reason for a DPO to take a decision for activating RED ALERT?

The Red Alert is activated in a very serious condition when it may not be possible for the Bessel to hold position. Some of the situations for activating Red Alert are.

- Vessel Drift off,

- Vessel Drive off,

- Possible failure of both DP networks,

- Collision with another vessel or a fixed structure

- Fire onboard or nearby vessel

28. What is an 'aging' blue in DP alarm light system?

Blue is an "Advisory" status. If after activating Blue advisory light, a risk assessment has been carried out and situation is considered to be acceptable and the job/mission may continue. This decision to continue the job/mission must be based on a good risk assessment and must be well documented.

29. In DP alarm status, what is a 'Proactive' yellow alert warning?

When the DPO on watch after considering a particular situation, decides to activate yellow alert. This particular situation may not be covered by the WSOG/ASOG, but the DPO with the situational awareness decided to move off as a proactive safe step.

30. In DP Operations an alarm status light, what is a reactive Yellow alert?

Based on the situational awareness and failures observed, If the DPO feels that next failure may be more damaging than the worst-case failure and may amount to a Red Alert. Basis this the DPO activates a Yellow status alert and this is usually referred to as Reactive Yellow Alert.

31. What is the purpose of online consequence analysis?

To carry out analysis that after a worst-case single point failure during operation, the online Consequence Analysis continually performs an analysis to check if the vessel is capable of holding her position and heading.

32. Why do some DP vessels have a software called online consequence analysis?

As per regulations, all DP vessels in class 2 and class 3 are required to have the online Consequence Analysis. This provision is to continually perform an analysis to check if the vessel is capable to hold position and heading after facing a single point failure.

33. What is the DP system function that performs calculations to check that sufficient thrust and power is available to maintain position and heading in the event of a single point failure?

    This special program installed on all the DP 2 and DP 3 vessels is called Consequence Analysis. The capability plot, as a result, can be used by the DP professional to check the capability of a dynamic positioning system.

34. What is dynamic positioning mobilization trial?

    DP trials wherein the vessel is being prepared for the task are called mobilization trials. These are a series of trials/checks/tests conducted as part of contact terms. The DP Mob trials are aimed at demonstrating the vessels capability for redundancy mainly and if any limitations for the same.

35. What is field arrival test for a DP vessel?

    DP vessel is hired to carry out certain task in the location agreed. The field trials are conducted to check if the vessel is performing good for those modes of DP operations and specific functions to be used while on the job.

36. What are Post DP Incident Trials?

    During the ongoing operations if a breakdown is observed on the DP system, appropriate corrective measures and required repairs must be carried out. On completion of these repairs a series to checks/trials are conducted to see if the vessel is safe for operations again.

37. What are the trails conducted after modification of vessels DP system?

    As per the IMCA guidelines stipulated on IMCA M 112, a series of checks are required after the vessels DP system has undergone a modification. The purpose of such tests and trials is mainly to assure if the vessel's position keeping performances are maintained/restored. It is observed in the industry that sometimes the names are different for these trials, but the purpose still remains the same.

38. What is DP FMEA trial?

Failure modes effects analysis, commonly known as FMEA are a set of test and checks which are mandatory for the class 2 and class 3 of DP vessels. These trails begin with the proving trials and thereafter repeated every year. The FMEA trials cover CAM or CAMO (critical activity mode of operation) and TAM the Task appropriate mode. These trial documents are one of the most important documents onboard a DP vessel and must be kept up to date including any modification or additions to the DP system.

39. What is DP FMEA proving trial?

The proving trials for FMEA are carried out initially to prove the DP system or after modifications to the DP system. Proving trails thereafter are repeated every five years. It is important that the findings of the initial proving trails and the subsequent repeat trials are recorded well, addressed and records for the same are kept onboard for reference.

40. Describe the DP annual trial?

DP vessels are tested annually for proving the performance as per standards. As an industry practice and guidelines from IMCA, the annual trails are permitted to be carried out with the three months duration of the due date. The three months can be before or after the due date. All earlier annual trails report must be kept onboard.

41. What are capability plots for a DP system?

    All DP 2 and DP 3 systems have a requirement to install a special feature called consequence analysis and capability plot. The plot is printed and kept for references. These plots can indicate the vessels capability to hold position and heading, under the given environmental conditions and with the stated set of equipment in service. Capability plots are saved for the future audits and trials.

42. List the steps followed in FMEA process.

    The whole process may be divided into various steps at certain stages. The stages are as below.

    - Starting Stage

    - Process stage

    - Completion/follow up stage

    During starting stage, the following steps may be required.

    - Identify and select a suitable team

    - After referring various inputs, define the standards to be followed

    - Decide on how the reporting procedures that will be followed.

    - Based on needs, define how deeper analysis to go into

    - Also important is to get the required system design and system information.

    During the FMEA process the following steps may be initiated.

    - Check and evaluate various failure modes and their effects on the DP system

- Look for the different methods to detect the failures and identify the corrective measures.

- Plan and make necessary arrangements for the vessel FMEA audit.

- Once agreed on schedule, arrange the physical audits in suitable location/s. This may be divided into different parts as per situations/. Some tests may be carried out in port and the others at sea in suitable weather conditions.

- Make a list of recommendations to be made for the above.

- Once the FMEA trials are completed the following may need to be planned.

- Formulate a suitable report as per the standards. This must include the observations and other recommendations in addition to the

- Insist on the follow up actions as promulgated and agreed.

43. What is a single point failure?

A single point failure is also known as common mode failure. For example, if a power supply which is common to two or three of the system/subsystem/components, may result in the failure of all such systems connected. A very famous example given more often is the failure of two valves for cooling system of a nuclear power plant in the US, resulting into a big accident. The common failure was the team/ group of engineers who maintained these valves. Sadly, both valves were not maintained appropriately, resulting into a common mode of failure.

Another example from the DP system may be failure of two similar network devices due to these being fitted in the same location and temperature of the compartment going high, resulting into complete failure of the DP system.

44. What are the main purposes of the FMEA analysis?

FMEA process is an attempt to answer the following questions.

- What is likely to go wrong with the DP system or the process being done using the DP system?

- If something/s going wrong, to what levels it may go to?

- What can be planned so that these breakdowns may be prevented?

These questions may look straight and simple but achieving this can be a task. So, a well planned and executed FMEA becomes a good tool.

45. What is endurance trial?

The endurance trial may be conducted on a new built vessel or after modifications/upgradation is carried out to check the ship under test is fit to undertake the DP operations under heavy load. Usually these tests last for about four hours and during this time no major alarms or situation must be observed.

46. What is upgradation trial or Modification Trial?

If the DP vessel have gone through a modification/alteration/upgradation, it is recommended to put the vessel through a trial, which is called a post modification trial or upgrade trial. These trials are based on the theme of FMEA trials to ensure that that the vessels concept of redundancy has not been affected.

47. What are main purposes of the DP vessels' footprints?

In general, the footprints of a DP vessel may serve the following purposes.

The footprints are able to give the scattering plot of the ship's position movements recorded at regular intervals. These movements are around the vessel's set position. Thus, the footprint gives the vessels position keeping accuracy.

The footprints also provide an indication of the environmental conditions the vessel may safely brave. This may imply that beyond these weather parameters, the vessel may not be able to hold position.

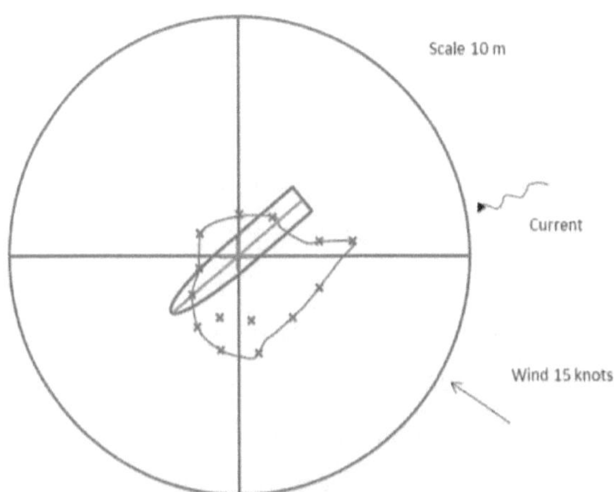

Fig: 12.3 Footprint

48. What scenarios must be included in the DP vessels capability plot?

It is recommended to include various scenarios of current of 0, 1 and 2 knots to test the vessels capability. The capability plots are plotted on polar plots. The following are considered.

- Case 1: What is the status when power and thruster fully operational

- Case 2: What happens when the most effective thruster is lost?

- Case 3: What happens after a worst-case failure has occurred?

49. Will the capability plot change if the current speed is increased?

The purpose of the vessel's capability plot is to calculate and present the vessels capability in maximum prevalent weather conditions. So, it is obvious that the capability plot will change. As the weather conditions are higher due to increase in the sea current, the capability of the vessel will be reduced.

50. What is the full power test on main engine or diesel generators?

This test aims at proving the full load capacity and load acceptance of the main engines and diesel generators. Engines are put to 100% load for a period of 15 minutes. (Of course, care must be taken in case the temperatures are rising dangerously) Once the temperatures stabilizes as expected the test is then completed in 15 minutes.

51. What is tunnel thruster full power trial?

This is testing of the thruster at full loads. It must test if there are alarms or unwanted shutdown of thruster. Set point and feedback must be compared at 100 % and maximum current drawn at 100% load.

52. What is independent joystick test?

The main purpose of this test is to see the operation of the independent joystick and verify that the DP operators are competent to use it if required.

53. In DP controls, what is Mathematical Model test?

   The purpose of this test is to check that the vessel holds position with the help of the ships mathematical model even after the loss of all the position reference sensors. After vessel has been in DP for more than 30 minutes, deselecting all the PRS, normally five minutes of observation to see if the vessel is holding position completes the test.

54. How do we test the position and heading warning and alarms?

   For testing the position and heading warning and alarms of the DP system, warning and alarm setting are usually set to a lower side. By using high gain, high speed and high rate of turning, initiate "Present Position and "Present Heading", observe the warning and alarms.

55. How do we test the gyro compass failure?

   Gyro failure can be tested by disconnecting the serial line interface to the DP controller. Once the line is disconnected, the concerned gyro failure alarm may be observed. Must revert the connections and confirm on completion of the test.

56. How do we test the gyro compass difference?

   Gyro difference alarm can be tested by using offset function at the sensor setting window. Insert an offset of around 3 degrees when the gyro is not enabled. Now enable and make this gyro as reference gyro. Gyro difference alarm may be observed now. Similar way, the other sensors may be disconnected and tested for failure. In the figure below, gyro #1 is frozen and rejected out.

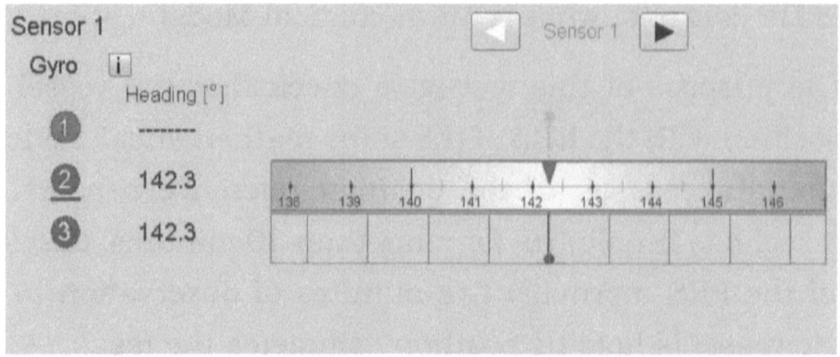

Fig 12.4   Gyro Compass Difference (courtesy Kongsberg)

57. How is DGNSS accuracy test carried out?

DGNSS accuracy test is carried out by selecting the particular DGPS and making a move @20 meters in all directions. Recommended speed of move is more than 0.5 Knot. It is expected that the maximum overshoot in this each 20-meter movement may not exceed 2 meters. Throughout the test

58. What are the main objectives of five yearly DP Renewal Trials?

The main objectives of the five yearly renewal trails are to ensure that the FMEA of the ship continues to be valid. The tests also are designed to check if all equipment including new machinery or equipment due to any upgrade are in good working condition and their response is as per the failure modes defined. These modes must have been included in the new trial's schedules.

These renewal trials when conducted, have to also help the ship staff for operations related issues by recognising how and where failures could occur thereby affecting the vessels position keeping capabilities. The onboard staff specially the operators get an opportunity to check their level of knowledge and understanding of the DP system in a controlled set of conditions so that even if there happens a failure in real situations, the safety of the ship is not compromised.

59. What must be the right action if there is a doubt about a test undertaken during DP FMEA trials?

Whenever there is any doubt about any test conducted, it is commonly acceptable process that the test must be repeated. The tests may be repeated only after an understanding about the same has been completed and everyone is accordingly prepared. The repeated test is not only aimed at the proving of redundancy of the power and thruster equipment but also to make use of the opportunity to prove that the operators are aware about the procedures and safe practices and display the necessary training and skills for the same.

60. How are the ER and Thruster room ventilation failure tests carried out?

The ventilation failure tests are carried out by shutting down the ventilation for 30 minutes for ER, thruster room, steering gear room, ECR, Switchboard, instrumentation room, bridge etc. The expected results are that the temperatures in the area should have a steady rise of temperature, no adverse effect to be observed. It is a common practice to note the temperature rise at 10, 20- and 30-minutes duration.

61. What is main purpose of full load trials of engines?

The main purpose of engine full load trials is to check and ensure engines are capable of full load. Test is carried out by keeping all thrusters online, loading the engines up to full load and holding for 15 minutes. If the temperature rises stabilised before that, test can be considered completed.

62. What is "software audit" in DP FMEA?

    Purpose of software audit is to record the software version installed in all DP related systems at the time of trials. It is also assumed that the software changes are updated before the audit. The following may be included.

    • DP Control Systems

    • DP OS

    • PMS

    • Thrusters and controls

    • Environmental sensors and PRS

63. During trials, how to demonstrate that the DP system can reject an erroneous Gyro reading?

    Prepare for testing by keeping the vessel on DP, keep the gyro to tested as the preference gyro.

    Using the offset function increase or decrease the heading till you observe the alarm – gyro rejected. After reverting back, see everything back to normal. Now disconnect the input signal for the gyro after identifying the same at the DP controller I/O devices. Observe appropriate alarm. On completion of the test, must revert back to normal ensuring proper connection.

64. Which programme or software cautions the DPO if the vessels lose capacity to withstand single worst failure?

    Consequences analysis is the software/programme which warns a DPO when there is loss of capability of the vessel. All the DP 2 and DP 3 vessels are required to have this programme. Online consequence analysis and the resultant capability plot are not a tool of planning, but these help the DPO take an appropriate decision.

65. **What may force a DP vessel lose class of operation?**

A DP vessel may lose her class of operation due to the change in weather parameters or loss of power, thruster, or switchboard. All these parameters are continuously tested and monitored by a software (online consequence analysis).

66. **Which components are monitored differently by DP system (other than the consequence analysis)?**

The important components which are monitored differently by DP system are as below.

- Failure of PRS

- Failure of controller

- Failure of OS

- Failure of sensors

67. **Having lost the class of DP, what action the DPO must initiate?**

Once the class of the agreed DP operations is lost, the DPO needs to:

- Activate amber alert.

- Inform master.

- Move to a safe location.

- Restore your class by repair/starting additional resources.

68. **What is purpose of "Consequence Analysis"?**

The purpose of consequence analysis is to monitor the redundancy of the vessel with regards to Power and

Thrusters. It warns the DPO when it finds that at the particular time if any of the active power bus, generator or thruster fails vessel will lose her heading and/or position. In other words, vessel's operation class will reduce to a lower class of DP. So, it may be observed that the main purpose of the consequence analysis is warming the DPO whenever the vessel degrades her operational class with regards to power and thruster.

69. What is purpose of "Capability Plot"?

Purpose of this plot is to give a theoretical measure to the operator about the capability of the vessel to withstand the environmental factor, the wind and or the current. In other words, with the systems in use up to what other conditions vessel will hold her heading and position. This information will be valuable to charters and masters about vessel's suitability for a particular purpose. Thus, we can clearly see that it is a planning tool which is used for planning an operation and is different in purpose from consequence which is not a planning tool but an operational tool used when an operation is ongoing.

70. What is purpose of "Footprint"?

The purpose of this plot is widely different from the previous two. This does not deal with the capability to withstand single worst failure and the vessel's capability to withstand certain amount of weather forces.

This plot gives us the vessel's performance report while keeping position. It indicates towards quality of position. Keeping in the form of how much she has been deviating from the position in a given situation. The performance is always about past and acts as a guide to present and future. The data may be irrelevant if it's too old. Therefore, this data is the form of a graphical plot is stored for future use.

This plot is not similar to capability plot but supplements the information given by capability plot. The capability plot tells us that the vessel has sufficient power and thrust available to withstand a given weather parameter, while foot-print plot tells us what the excursion of the vessel will be while keeping position in given weather condition. Thus, we can say that footprint is also a planning tool.

CHAPTER 13

COMMUNICATION AND DOCUMENTATION

1. What is the document for reference regarding operational communication on board offshore/DP vessels?

    IMCA document (Marine 205 and Diving 046) are the standard references for the communication during various operations. The figure below depicts a typical set of communication channels for various activities the vessel may be engaged in.

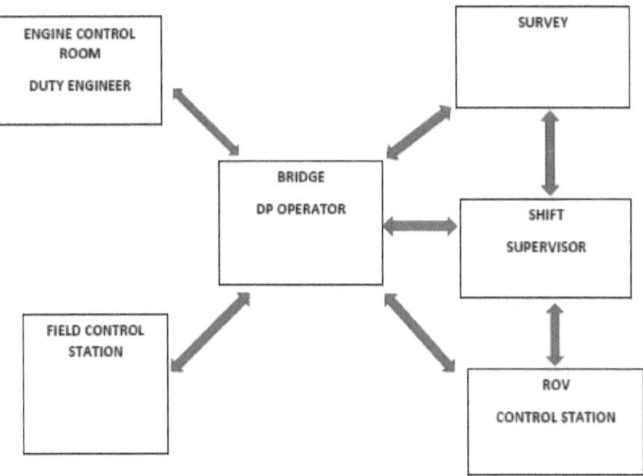

Fig: 13.1 Typical Communication Arrangements

2. What are important components of operational communication between the vessel and the platform especially for operational changes?

Every DP working in a field is expected to inform the field controller the following when a change is expected/has taken place in the operational status (but not restricted to);

- Vessel coming into 500 meters zone or leaving

- Vessel setting up DP system

- Vessel comes and setup in location

- If applicable, four-point mooring operations start and finish, unmooring start and finish.

- About the diving bell going up and down

- Diver gone out or returned

- Beginning and end of surface diving

- Starting and finishing of ROV operations

- All crane activities

It is particularly important that the local area conditions and requirements must be kept in mind during al operations.

3. What all may be included in the communication from Dive control to DP control?

Generally, the communication/update from the "Dive Control" to bridge may include the following.

- Status of the diving bell

- Status of diver/s

- Plan to use water jet

- Equipment used in water jetting

- Diving bell or other equipment which may create hinderance for underwater equipment and position reference sensors.

- All down-lines and their status

- Any condition or situation which result in any change to the earlier agreed procedures.

4. What all may be included in the communication from DP control to Dive Control?

Communication between the bridge and the dive control station is critically important.

Bridge/DP control would generally like to keep the dive control station always updated about the following.

- Intended move of vessel or her heading.

- Operational status changes which may affect ships position control

- Any other unusual situation due to which the agreed procedures may have to change

- Weather forecast

- Actual changes in weather conditions

- Other vessels moving in vicinity

- Any plan to handle downlines

- Operation of Tautwire and its weight

- Launching/recovery of HPR transducer and beacons

- This update must be passed onto the divers accordingly by the dive control.

5. Describe the general communication between engine control room (ECR) to Bridge/DP Control.

There is a lot and particularly important communication between the ECR to bridge.

This may include the following (but not limited to).

- Intention, approval and continuance of already approved work under permit to work.

- Completion of work as reported by ECR.

- All info and advice about any system electrical/mechanical which may have intervention due to such work as approved and that is likely to affect the DP system online/in use or standby whether intentionally or unintentionally.

- Starting or stopping, or intention thereof, of ancillary pneumatic and hydraulic system.

- Any other system, starting/stopping of which may reduce pressure on DP or diving related equipment.

- Bilge or ballast water pumping/intention to pump overboard.

- Plan or intention to start/stop any equipment which may directly or indirectly affect the power management system or DP control system.

- Starting/intentions to start any equipment which may affect ship's trim.

- Any failure or fault condition which may fault affect ships redundancy/capability.

6. Describe the general communication between Bridge/DP Control and engine control room (ECR).

   Bridge/DP control being the nerve centre of the ship, would like to have continuous updates from the ECR and thus the communication may include the following.

   - Requirement of additional power/starting of generators.

   - Vessel setting up on location

   - Launch of ROV or divers in water.

   - Any move of the vessel which may need additional power

   - Any change in weather conditions.

   - All matters related to trim and list and all ballasting or de-ballasting activities.

   - All operations on deck such as crane or heavy lifting.

   - Starting and completion of location check list.

7. What all may be part of communication between the platform/fixed structure and the DP vessel working nearby?

   There is very vital information exchange between the platform and the DP vessel/s working nearby and may include the following.

   - Any movements of vessels and helicopters in near vicinity.

   - Any activity like crane lift etc. which is likely to affect the ROV or diving operations.

   - Any activity or crane movements on surface/subsea which may block the position reference sensors.

   - Any planning or real discharge affecting underwater activities.

- All issues related to blackout of power or communication.

- All operations/activities which may be hazardous underwater (well testing etc)

- Updated weather information.

- Any subsea operations nearby.

- Location of functional or abandoned underwater HPR beacons.

- Any adjustment for the mooring lines specially in case of a moored structure.

8. What kind of information exchange takes place between the DP control and the platform?

   A DP vessel operating near to a fixed structure is expected to communicate the following.

   - Divers and the status, any change in status.

   - DP system status, any changes in the status.

   - All operations which may use some hazardous tools/ activities.

   - A change in position/heading beyond certain limits as per the operational guidelines.

9. What are the main features of the communication onboard a drilling vessel?

   The main features of the communication onboard a DP drill ship is that there must be a frequent and regular contact between the drilling station, bridge and the engine control room. Quick and clear communication helps in ensuring that the action taken by one station is understood and appropriate measures are initiated accordingly by the other stations as well. All communication must be clear and be acknowledged as per the guidelines.

10. List out the communication items from ROV Control to DP Control.

    ROV control/ROV Shack is expected to communicate the following to bridge or to the DP Control station.

    • Permission to launch ROV.

    • ROV leaving ship, in water and then what depth.

    • When ROV surfaces on completion of task or otherwise.

    • Any change/loss in communication with ROV.

    • Any other safety issue for ROV operations.

11. What are the main features of the communication between the control station of DP (Bridge) to control station of ROV?

    The bridge must communicate the following to the ROV control.

    • Permission to launch ROV granted.

    • The current situation and location of the underwater lines which also includes the Tautwire.

    • All obstruction to ROV due to any down-lines.

    • Any of the hardware including the beacons of HPR which may cause hinderances to the movements of ROV.

    • Any change in the positions of transponder beacons.

    • Vessels heading or position change.

    • Status by using the DP alert system. It may be noted that the most important means of communication between these stations is the DP alert system.

12. What is DP Alert System?

    DP Alert System is a method of communication from bridge to various locations to give warning of degradation of the DP system or of the vessel's ability to continue the operation for the following locations for example; Diving/ROV control, drilling, pipe laying or other critical operation.

13. What are the precautions to be taken while working on VHF/UHF Channels during operational communication?

    - While arriving on location, check and communicate with the controller of the field.

    - Keep a watch to continuously monitor the agreed channel.

    - Monitor the channel continuous

    - Follow strictly the radio procedures as laid by the control

    - Always observe safe distance between DP equipment and UHF handset.

    - Must follow guidelines for use of mobile phone during operations.

    - Use Standard Marine Communication Phrases (SMCP) in all communications.

14. What precautions must be observed during emergency communications?

    While in an emergency situation, ensure that all unnecessary communication systems and channels should be switched off. This will help to make sure that there is a direct communication between the personnel/stations involved in an emergency.

15. What does Standard Marine Communication Phrases (SMCP) recommend for effective communication?

    SMCP recommends using clear communication and certain words/phrases to be avoided. Pay attention not to use words like May, Might, Should, Could etc. Refer SMCP for details.

16. What is DP Check list?

    DP checklist are a series of documents (once completed) to confirm the readiness of the DP system for the operations.

17. What is DP Location Set Up Checklist?

    When the vessel arrives in location to carry out the job assigned, certain checklists must be completed. These are called the DP Location Set Up Checklists. The purpose of these checklists is to indicate that ships setting up process in location is a s per the procedures.

18. What is so important about the Pre -Diving e Checklist?

    Before preparing for diving operations onboard a diving support vessel, a series of checks are required to be completed. These checks are to ensure that the diving operations are carried out safely. Communication plays a big role in safety critical operations and hence all main and back up communications must be checked.

19. What are engine control room (ECR) Checklists for DP operations?

    These check list include various checks and test to ensure that the setting up of various machinery to be used for DP operations are done as per procedures and the configuration of the systems is done appropriately for the jobs. The critical activity mode (CAM) and task appropriate mode guidance is followed.

20. What are the checks included in the 500m Check List for a DP vessel?

    When the DP vessel is preparing to arrive and enter the 500 meter zone as series of checks and tests are carried out. The purpose of the checks and test is to ensure safe operations by preparing well for the same. On completion of these checks the same are reported to the asset manager. An approval to enter the 500 meter zone is then given by the asset manager so that the vessel can make movements closer to the rig for the operations. All channels of communication and the back are also tested for this.

21. What is watch changeover status or the six hourly checklist for a DP vessel?

    Watch changeover status or the six hourly checklists include a number of tests and checks which needs to be carried out by the watch keeping DP operator. The purpose of these checks and test is to ensure that the setting up and functioning of the DP system is as per standard procedures.

22. List the records that needs to be maintained so that the same are easily accessible for use by the ship staff and the other parties concerned?

    All DP vessels are required to prepare and maintain the following records for the ship staff and the other interested parties. Small variations here and there may be due to vessels specific operational requirements.

    - Reports for Annul DP trails, DP FMEA and FMEA proving trials reports

    - All DP related check list for the engine room and the bridge.

- All incident reports and investigations of the same followed by the closing reports.

- Faults and breakdown of DP system and related equipment, records of repairs carried out, any modification etc.

- Vessel specific training programmes and familiarisation for the DP professionals who join ship for a short period.

- Training programmes for the main DP professionals for their development.

- Print outs of alarms as required and all the necessary logbooks.

- Reports and updates from the vendors for the DP system

- TAGOS, CAMO, TAM AND ASOG/WSOG

- Prints of consequence analysis and capability plots, DP footprints for different situations.

- Any other specific documents as advised by the class/ charter/oil major.

23. Describe the planned maintenance program for a DP vessel.

Due to the safety requirements on board DP vessel, the planned maintenance must be carried out and specifically address the DP system components. IMCA document M 109 gives more details and may be referred to for this. DP system planned maintenance must include all these equipment which in turn may have an effect on the position keeping capability of the vessel. Records for all these must be maintained.

24. What is main purpose of testing communication during the annual DP trials?

The purpose is to ensure that there are good communications between all locations. Testing of all available communications between Bridge, ECR, Engine Room, Thruster Rooms and other relevant machinery spaces.

25. Name the documents which are checked during the DP vessel FMEA trails?

The following documents may be checked during the FMEA trials.

- Vessel footprints

- Capability plots

- DP checklists and last filled in

- ASOG/WSOG

- CAMO

- SIMOPS documents

- DP operations manual

- DP FMEA

- DP Annual Trials

- DP Incident reports

- Vendor maintenance reports

- Vendor supplied drawings

- DP drawings

- DP one-line and I/O list available in DP cabinet(s)

- Labels inside cabinets and/or on UPS permanently affixed

26. What may be the general communication arrangement onboard a DP vessel?

A general communication arrangement may vary from vessel to vessel depending upon the operational activity requirements. However, a generic arrangement will include communication from bridge to all other stations of operation and machinery control. The same is depicted in Fig 13.1.

CHAPTER 14

DP PERSONNEL AND THEIR RESPONSIBILITIES

1. What is the traditional hierarchical structure of a DP vessel management?

The traditional hierarchical structure onboard a DP vessel may vary a little, depending upon the task assigned, region of deployment/client, the class of the vessel. The diagram below explains the typical hierarchical flow chart of a DP vessel.

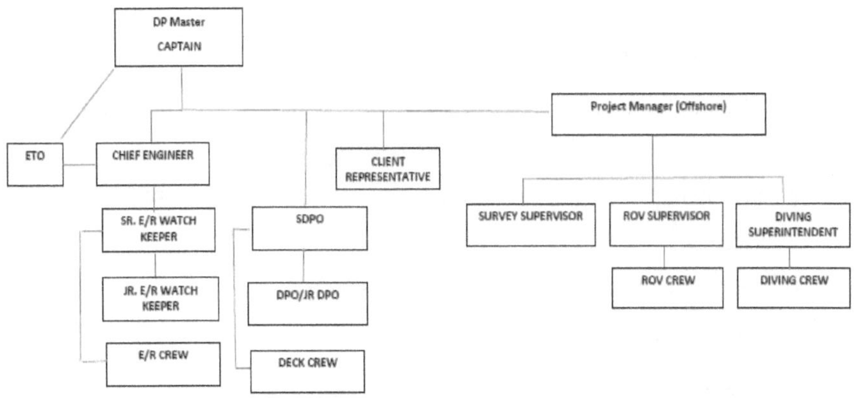

Fig: 14.1   Typical hierarchical flow chart of a DP vessel

2.   What are the responsibilities of a Chief Engineer on board offshore/DP vessels?

The Chief Engineer should hold a valid Certificate of Competency equivalent to an approved and current Standards of Training, Certification and Watchkeeping (STCW) convention standard. The Chief Engineer should have a full understanding and knowledge of the power, thruster and sensors for the DP operational requirements. The knowledge must be utilized for proper understanding of the failures and the consequences of the failure on the operations.

Additionally, it is important that CE leads the engine room team in establishing proper communication with the bridge team. CE must also be aware of the vessels operations manual and procedures and possesses good knowledge about the ships FMEA.

3.   What are the responsibilities of a watch keeping engineer on board offshore/DP vessels?

The senior engine room watchkeepers should hold a valid Certificate of Competency. As per approved current STCW convention standard. the senior engine room watchkeepers should have a full understanding of the vessels dynamic positioning operational requirements. The watch keeping engineers must also have knowledge about the consequences of failures and should be able to optimize the redundancy available in the DP system and all related equipment.

Additionally, the senior engine room watchkeepers should understand the importance of communications between the bridge and engine control room. Good understanding and knowledge of the ships operations manuals which includes the important documents like the FMEA which must have been updated.

4. What are the responsibilities of an Electrical Officer/ETO on board offshore/DP vessels?

Electrical officers should be assessed for competence according to A-III/6 of the STCW code. The ETO or electrical officer as may be designated, must competent and should have good understanding of the ships DP controls including the sensors, position reference sensors, thruster and the power system.

ETO should be capable of understanding the DP system and related equipment in such a way that he can easily carry out all checks, tests and maintenance on the DP equipment. The responsibilities also include routine checks and special checks carried out for special occasions and trials. ETO must be quite familiar with the communication between ER/Bridge and other operational areas. Good knowledge of the operational manual and FMEA trails will help the ETO to understand the job assigned well to facilitate the various test and trials. Repair/replacement of components in DP related equipment forms an important part of the ETO's job responsibilities. ETO must understand that while carrying out any of these checks/test must not inadvertently cause the loss of redundancy in the DP system.

5. What are the responsibilities of DP Master on board offshore/DP vessels?

The captain or Master/DP Master should hold, as a minimum, a Class 1 (Deck/Master) Certificate of Competency or equivalent to an approved current STCW convention standard. Master should also have a DP operator certificate issued by the Nautical Institute or other schemes as may be acceptable by various companies. The Master should be trained, competent, sufficiently experienced and knowledgeable with the class of vessel to the satisfaction of the company. Minimum experience for the Master may vary depending upon the type of vessel and company to company.

In addition to the above, the DP Master should be competent and experienced to carry out and assist during the annual DP trails of the vessel and the DP FMEA trails of the vessel. The captain must display skills that he/she can train, assess and guide the other DP staff accordingly.

6. What are the responsibilities of DP operator on board offshore/DP vessels?

A dynamic positioning operator (DPO) is trained and competent seafarer as per the guideline's requirements given in the section 6.3.2 of IMCA M 117 – The Training and Experience of Key DP Personnel. DPOS additionally must have completed the training schemes as promulgated by the Nautical Institute London. All qualified DPOs must be competent enough to take care of the DP watchkeeping duties independently and assist the master in all DP related tests and trails. Additionally, the DPOS must be able to train and guide the junior DPOs and trainees as per ships requirements.

7. What are the responsibilities of junior DP operator on board offshore/DP vessels?

A junior dynamic positioning operator (JDPO) may be the suitable trained and qualified officer onboard, A junior DPO must meet the requirements as per the guidelines and requirements given in the IMCA M 117.

8. What are the responsibilities of a senior DP operator on board offshore/DP vessels?

A senior DPO (SDPO) may be defined as the qualified as per the competence requirements outlined in IMCA M117. SDPO is meeting or exceeding the company specified requirements in the number of hours of DP watch keeping and qualifications. SDPO must be able to lead the team of DP watch keepers and hold the vessel in position while on the DP assignments. They must also be able to guide and train the junior DP operators as per the company guidelines and the requirements.

9. What is the importance of DP maintenance staff onboard a DP vessel?

DP maintenance staff would generally be designated as the Chief Engineer and electrical officer although it is beneficial and a good practice to also have appropriately trained senior engine room watchkeepers. DP maintenance staff is expected to have acquired adequate knowledge about the ships DP equipment. This can be done by attending the required DP training. The training these days should be as per the Nautical Institute guidelines. Type specific/ship specific training wherever required may be attained as per the client/job requirements

All maintenance staff may use IMCA logbook and all trainings may be logged in the book. The training and experience attained by the DP maintenance staff helps the vessel in making sure that the faults and breakdowns are attended to in the most efficient way and the breakdown and off hires may be brought down to minimum or be avoided.

10. What is DP Planned Maintenance?

    All DP enabled ships should have a well-structured planned maintenance system that specifically. IMCA document, IMCA M109 may be referred to for more details. Vessels' planned maintenance programmes must include all equipment which may have an impact on the vessel's station keeping capabilities. Ideally, this must include power systems, distribution system, switchboard, bustie breakers for the powering the thruster.

    Thrusters and propulsion systems must also be included. The sensors and position reference sensors being an important part of the DP system, should also have a planned maintenance schedule so that the required checks and test must be carried out. This should include indirect components such as generator circuit breakers, bus tie breakers, etc. Maintenance should include regular cleaning, calibration, and testing of equipment as outlined in manufacturer's recommendations and industry guidelines. All planned and unplanned maintenance be recorded as per the company procedures and be ready for the audit as and when required.

    Maintenance may require replacement of certain parts. So, it is also advisable the vessel maintains the minimum number of the required spares. Most vessels and companies follow a well-maintained inventory which may be suitable linked to the maintenance program. Adequate inventory and proper maintenance may help the vessel getting back to working status sooner after a DP incident or a failure.

11. What happens when a thruster fault occurs?

    A thruster which has reported a fault may not respond like a normal thruster. The DP commands may not be executed, or feedback may be wrong. Both will create further problems. Here an important role to be played by the DPO that he/she must identify the faulty thruster and use emergency stop to bring the situation under control at the earliest and not allowing it to deteriorate further.

12. What is the appropriate action from the DPO when a DP operators station fails?

In the event of an operator station failing, the DP operators must take controls on the standby operator station. During this period, the DP system performance to maintain the vessels heading and position must not be affected.

13. During operations, the duty engineers gets an alarm for cooling water "Low Pressure". What is the appropriate action?

The duty engineer may try to change over the sea chest valve and see if the cooling water pressure is back to normal. May be the earlier sea chest valve got blocked, appropriate actions may be initiated to ensure redundancy is maintained.

14. Why is it so difficult to identify a faulty thruster when it has failed to full thrust?

When a thruster fails to full thrust, it becomes difficult to identify which thruster has failed. This due to the fact that under such situations, the other thrusters also will pick up extra load to compensate the effects of the failed thruster. The best thing to be done under such circumstances by the operator or engineer is to identify the thruster whose command and feedback signals are not matching. Usually this the best bet to identify the faulty or runaway thruster.

15. In a diesel electric propulsion vessel, what can be done to save the vessel from blackout when fuel control system is misbehaving, and switchboards are connected together/ bustie closed?

    In such a situation when the bustie is closed and the fuel control system of a generator is misbehaving, the duty engineer must be able to save a full blackout by opening bustie and containing the blackout only one side of the switchboard (partial blackout). A similar situation may be created by other faults such as problem with a generator excitation.

16. What is the most appropriate action for the DPO when on a DP3 vessel the main controller has failed?

    In such a situation, the DPO must changeover command to the backup DP system, which is installed in an A/60 bulkhead area and maintain the vessels position till safe termination of the ongoing operation.

17. What action should the DPO take to ensure timely weather updates?

    The DP on watch must make use of ships radars prudently to keep a track of weather changes such as squalls approaching. This help him to maintain the DP in good condition by initiating timely action to have standby power and thruster or change heading as precautionary measure.

18. In case the power to a thruster is from two sources (auto changeover), what precautions and additional action must the duty engineer take in a situation when there is power failure in one section?

    The duty engineer must be able to identify the auto changeover thruster and check if the auxiliaries for the same thruster are fed from which power source. If need be, change over the auxiliaries to the source available (may be manually)

19. What is the safety in DP system against the drive off due to a faulty position reference sensor/s?

   As per the class rules, a DP 2 or DP 3 vessel will be installed with minimum three reference sensors and two will be of different principles of operation. This provides a position calculation errors due to a common failure mode. Also, DPO with the help of DP computer can identify the PRS which is malfunctioning and deselect the same immediately, so that the faulty PRS doesn't affect the position keeping capability of the vessel.

20. What precaution do the engineers must exercise while handling a fuel leak in a "common fuel supply system"?

   It is good practice to manually change over a fuel filter so that all generators are not affected.

21. On vessel with only two gyro compasses, the DPO gets an alarm for heading difference. What is best way to handle this situation?

   The DPO must identify the faulty gyro and select the good one for use otherwise the heading change will be uncontrollable.

22. The vessel is fitted with two wind sensors. The DPO observes a wind sensor difference alarm. What is the most advisable action?

   The DPO must make a decision which is the good wind sensor. It may be a possibility that one of the wind sensors may have failed due to quick change of wind speed.

The DPO must identify the faulty sensor and deselect the same otherwise vessels heading will start changing very quickly.

23. What is the statement of competence of key DP personnel onboard?

The statement of competence of the key DP personnel onboard is a document prepared by the master to indicate that the key DP personnel have the required standards of competency as per the IMCA M 117 (Guidelines for The Training and Experience of Key DP Personnel). Masters may be authorized by his/her company to withdraw the statement as and when it may be felt that the concerned DP personnel does not meet the sated requirements.

CHAPTER 15
DP OPERATIONS

1. What may be source/s of hazard while carrying out diving operations from a DP vessel?

    The vessel is maintained in auto DP mode for the diving operations by using its thrusters. The continuously running thrusters are a potential hazard for divers & umbilical cord of the divers. But this drawback is overcome by the safety standards provided by the DP system.

2. What is Universal Transverse Mercator (UTM)? Where do we use this?

    Universal transverse Mercator (UTM) is a process assigning coordinates to a specific position. The UTM coordinates uses the premises of dividing the earth into sixty zones of six degrees each. Zone number one starts from the international date line i.e. 180 degrees and covers up to 174 degrees west. Position of the vessel in UTM coordinates is indicated in meters. Degrees are converted in meters using trigonometrical and geometrical calculations. The Figure below depicts UTM selected and position indicated in meters.

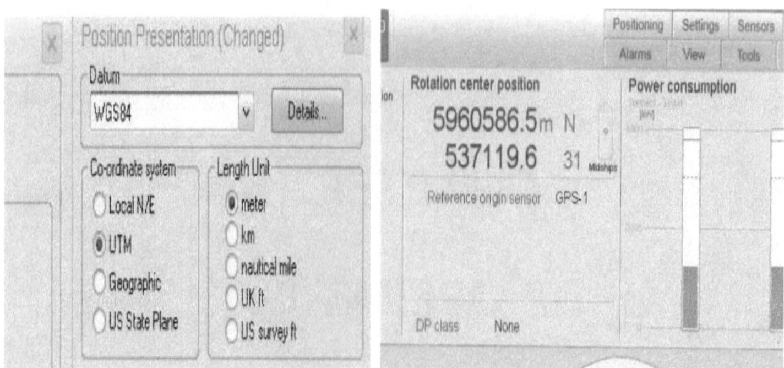

Fig: 15.1   Universal Transverse Mercator (UTM) – (Courtesy – Kongsberg)

3.   What are "False Easing" and "False Northing"

In DP system view options for the position presentation have choice to activate "False Easting" and "False Northings" as required. False easting is always selected and for this a figure of 500000 is used to replace the central meridian zero value. This value of 500000 is used to ensure that even when the vessel moves westwards from the central meridian, the position values will not be negative.

False northing is only activated when the vessel is working in the southern hemisphere. When this is activated, a value of 10million 800 is used to represent the equator zero value. Using this value ensures that the position value will never go to negative while in southern hemisphere.

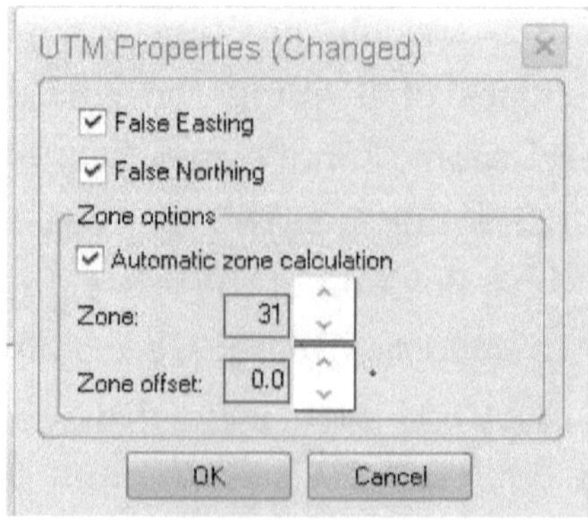

Fig: 15.2   False Easing/False Northing (Courtesy Kongsberg)

4. What is most important feature of a DP system set to the 'Auto Position' mode?

    By putting the vessel in Auto DP mode, the vessel's position and heading can be maintained as closely as possible to the set-point values, which otherwise, is not so easy to achieve.

5. What are the disadvantages of a ship (utilizing its DP system) compared to using anchors while working?

    The major disadvantage is the continually running thrusters which are must for a vessel on DP. These continuously running thrusters may pause hazards for divers and ROVs working underwater.

6. How is the Equipment Class necessary for a particular operation decided?

    The Equipment Class/Redundancy required for a particular operation should be decided after carrying out a full risk assessment of the proposed operation. The risk assessment may be carried out jointly by the owner of the vessel and the charterer.

7. Why is it necessary that the DP operator must be familiar with the details of the worksite?

    The DP operator must be able to identify the hazards involved in a particular operation. For this he must also plan the contingencies. To ensure all these, it is necessary for a DPO to be familiar with all the details of worksite.

8. During DP operations, if a warning message is received which indicates that there will be insufficient thrust if you lose a certain thruster group. What options would be best in this situation?

    It is advisable that the DPO evaluate the prevailing environmental forces and change heading/position if possible, during the operations under process.

9. A DP-capable vessel is engaged in ROV operations. The DP system is selected into 'Follow-Sub' or 'Follow-Target mode'. The operator is able to select a value known as 'React radius' or 'Operational radius'. What is this value?

   This value known as Reaction radius or Operational Radius of the vessel is the distance the ROV can move freely for doing the task. If the ROV moves beyond the defined RADIUS, the vessel will move using thruster and position herself in the centre of the circle.

10. A DP-capable drilling rig is engaged in drilling operations in deep water. The DP system is selected into 'Riser Angle Mode' for positioning. Position reference is from dual DGPS and an acoustic system. Explain, how riser angle data is provided?

    The sensors placed on the flex joints measure the angle and send the same to the DP controller. Based on the angle, the distance of movement is calculated, and appropriate thrust is then applied using online thrusters.

11. In which "Mode" the DPO can use the DP system to achieve automatic change of position or heading?

    Automatic control of vessels position (surge and sways movements) and heading (Yaw movement) is possible only in "Auto Position" or "Auto DP" mode.

12. Which of the following inputs is required before surge or sway can be automatically controlled?

    To control the surge and sway movements of the vessel, these movements are required to be measured. The sensor which measures the surge and sway are called the position reference sensor (PRS) or position measuring equipment (PME).

13. Which DP sensor measure roll and pitch?

    The sensors which measures the roll and pitch is known as vertical reference unit (VRU) or vertical reference sensor (VRS). The modern sensor which can measure roll pitch and heave are known as motions reference unit or MRU.

14. On a PSV alongside an installation a sudden high unexpected increase of DP current (Residual Force) is observed. What is the most probable reason?

    This could be due to an error in the wind sensor. As the vessel is close to a rig, and the wind senor may be partially sheltered or the windage are of the vessel may be partially sheltered. This may result in the wind model getting affected badly and hence an unexpected increase in the residual forces.

15. Why is it important to check the center of rotation (COR) prior to using the DP system?

    The default setting of COR is midships (CG). If the COR is set incorrectly the vessel may maneuver unexpectedly,

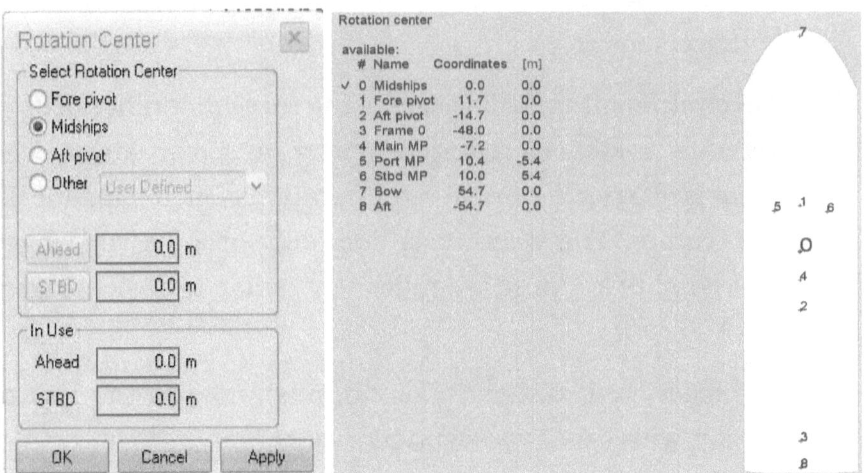

Fig: 15.3   Centre of Rotation (COR) Courtesy Kongsberg

As shown above the centre of rotation is selected "Midship". Depending upon the requirements the COR may be selected by the DP operator accordingly.

16. Suppose a vessel is on DP, close to a platform structure hidden in the leeway side. A single wind Sensor is selected. What will happen to the vessel if the wind sensor is suddenly exposed to the wind, but the hull and superstructure is still in wind shadow?

    The system will apply thrust and move against the wind. As the sensor is suddenly exposed to the wind, it will measure the correct wind, but the wind is still not working on the super structure. This may result in violent movements of the vessel.

17. Which DP mode allows a DP vessel to automatically follow an ROV?

    Follow ROV or follow target mode is used when it is required the DP vessel to follow a submerged target, usually an ROV. The ROV will have a beacon (Responder) installed on the top which will be used by the ships HiPAP/HPR system as the reference sensor.

18. A DP equipment class 2 vessel using three different position reference systems, required power and thrusters. The vessel is carrying out diving operations on a pipeline in open waters. The weather is suddenly become very foggy and visibility reduced significantly, what are the biggest risks?

    The biggest risk under these circumstances is the risk of collision with other vessels underway.

19. How important is the weather forecast as a factor in DP operations?

    The weather forecast is very important factor for all DP operations. It should be included in both the Pre DP checks and watch handover checklist. Continuous weather forecast must also be checked for better planning.

20. A DP Class 2 vessel, on a DP class charter, fitted with two bow tunnels and two azimuths on the stern. If one azimuth thruster is out of service due to some reason, what will be the effect of this on DP operations?

    Upon losing the thruster, the DPO must have a look at the consequence analysis and the capability plot, prepare to pull out of location safely if the vessel is not capable. The vessel may no longer be safe to continue the operations in DP class 2 requirements.

21. On a Class 2 vessel, working with two switch boards, bus tie open condition. What actions would the DPO initiate if there is a blackout on one side due to shorting in the switchboard?

    The DPO must prepare to pull out of location safely. The vessel is no longer safe to continue the operations in DP class 2 requirements.

22. A DP class 2 vessel when working close to another DP vessel, what may be the causes of potential mutual interference?

    The potential interreference may be due to thruster wash resulting in high DP current/residual current. Also, there may be interference from the acoustic reference sensor mutually. GPS reception may also be affected due to multipath error(reflection).

23. If a DP vessel, working inside 500 meters, the DPO observes that the vessel has lost redundancy. What action must the DPO initiate?

    The DPO/SDPO/Master must declare the yellow alert, abandon operations safely and move the vessel to a safe location before attempting to revive the redundancy.

24. When planning a DP operation, what is most essential part?

    It very essential part of any planning that a full hazard-identification and risk assessment be conducted. If the risks/hazards are within the accepted limits the operations may be safely undertaken. If not risk management process must be undertaken on mitigate the risks.

25. A vessel has completed her approach to a worksite which is close alongside a fixed platform. She is in her final working position. Before giving the 'green light' allowing the start of ROV operations what is more important?

    On arrival location and before starting the job it is essential that the vessel must be allowed to settle down in location for at least thirty minutes. This is to endure safe operations.

26. Before entering the 500-metre platform exclusion zone in order to conduct DP operations, what is considered very important?

    For all operation risk assessment is very important step. So, contingency planning to establish vessel escape routes must have been completed before entering 500-meter zone.

27. The 'Weathervane' or 'Auto Heading Select' facility is an essential function in which type of operations?

    These modes of operations are generally available and applied for shuttle tanker/FPSO or offshore loading operations.

28. During diving operations from a diving support vessel on DP, how the length of the diver's umbilical must be managed.

    The safety of diver is very important. He must never be allowed to proceed near to a running thruster. For this purpose, the length of umbilical cord is never allowed so that diver can never reach closer than five meters to the nearest thruster.

29. A PSV working alongside a rig suddenly experiences a sudden rise in DP current/residual current. Just before some time there was an alarm for a thruster pitch feedback. Are these two related??

    Yes, these are related alarms. The thruster pitch feedback alarm resulted in a difference of thrust required and thrust applied. Due to this after some time the current (Residual Force) increase is observed. In a way this indicates the failure of the thruster as there is huge difference between command and feedback. Emergency stop for this thruster must be activated.

30. About what point does a DP vessel rotate when changing heading?

    The centre of rotation (COR) as selected by the DP operator will decide where the vessel will rotate from. The default COR is the CG of the ship. But COR may be required to be selected from other locations depending upon the type to job the vessel is doing.

31. When moving a DP vessel from one work location to the other, what waypoint would you recommend using?

    For safe practices, the DPO must select a waypoint that will be outside the 500-meter zone of the next work location.

32. What is important before entering the 500m zone for safe DP operations?

    For safe DP operations, it is important that contingency planning to plan an escape route has been completed. Other check lists etc. will have to be completed as a procedure.

33. A DP ROV vessel working in deep waters, which of the DP Position Reference Systems (PRS) could the ROV possibly interfere with?

    The ROV during its maneuvers may interfere/entangle with Taut wire and HPR transponders. The ROV control and DPO must keep a good communication to avoid such occurring.

34. A DP vessel with 2 tunnels thrusters forward, 2 tunnel thrusters aft, 2 main engines/propellers/rudders. Main propellers are pitch control type. During DP operations the Port main propeller fails to full ahead pitch causing a drive off towards nearby platform. What should the DPOs do?

    The first and important thing to be done by the DPO is to identify the failed thruster/propeller and activate emergency stop at the earliest.

35. What are standard or in practice uses of DP class 2 vessels?

    As a well-accepted practice DP 2 vessels are in use for the following types of offshore.

    Drilling, diving, pipelay, umbilical lay, lifting, accommodation barges (outside 500 metre), shuttle tanker offtake, ROV support (Close proximity - Surface/subsea), well stimulation and logistic vessels.

36. A per IMO/MSC 1580, what are the new requirements for DP operation manual?

    The following checklists, test procedures, trials and instructions should be incorporated into the vessel-specific DP Operations Manuals:

    - Location checklist

    - Watchkeeping checklist

    - DP operating instructions

    - Annual tests and procedures

    - Initial and periodical (5-year) tests and procedures

    - Examples of tests and procedures after modifications and non-conformities

    - Blackout recovery procedure

    - List of critical components

    - Examples of operating modes

    - Decision support tools such as ASOG

    - Capability plots

37. What must be taken into consideration before planning an operational activity?

    Before planning an operational activity, it is always recommended to look into the following.

    - Look for and define the ships DP systems and other equipment configuration, in relation to the activity and location/weather. This can be seen in the critical activity mode (CAMO) task appropriate mode (TAM).

- Based on the activity specific operating guidelines (ASOG), define various limits for equipment in relation with the operational parameters for the location.

- Define what needs to be done by the key personnel onboard, when a fault occurs, or the performance of the equipment deteriorate.

Appropriate guidance notes can be compiled to be used by the vessel team in a very user friendly manner so that these guidance notes may be referred to by the bridge, deck, engine and other staff, when an operational activity is being planned.

38. Describe activity specific operating guidelines (ASOG) in simple words.

ASOG may be simply described as an operational document presenting activity in four categories as mentioned below.

- Green: Green status indicated that the normal operations in progress. DP system working normal and operations can be carried out in safe and agreed manner.

- Advisory (Blue): The advisory blue light indicates that though risks are there, but operations may continue while the risks are being analysed. The risks could be due to equipment or weather limits approaching.

- Yellow: The yellow or warning status indicates that there is some problem that requires that the operations may have to be suspended, cause/s to be investigated. The problem/s may be due to loss of redundancy and any failure further may result in the loss of vessel's position or heading or both. The warning status may also indicate that the operational limits have been reached or the limits for the performance of the equipment or the weather parameters are crossed.

- Red: The red status is a situation wherein an emergency state is indicated, which may require the immediate stopping of vessel operations. This could be due to system failure, environmental conditions or any other emergency situation like fire or flooding in a compartment.

39. What needs to be considered for planning and developing ASOG?

The team planning and developing an ASOG, must consider the following.

- Look at the ships critical activity mode of operation (CAM).

- Is the vessel suitable, technically, to carry out the job?

- Study the vessels position keeping capabilities carefully and what happens after a worst-case failure has taken place.

- Must take into consideration the existing environmental conditions, looking at the job and the location.

40. Explain what the critical activity mode (CAM) table contains?

A CAM table must include the green i.e. normal operation criteria and the blue i.e. advisory status criteria.

41. What are the recommended operational documents for DP?

The vessel owner/operators are expected to have the following (but not limited to) documents.

- FMEA/FMECA report for the vessel

- Proving trails for FMEA

- DP FMEA annual trials

- Capability plots recorded at various occasions

- Footprints of the DP

- Service engineers reports for DP related systems

- Any modification or additions to DP system

- Audit/DP audit reports

- Ship Specific DP operations manual

- Incidents reports for DP

- All DP check list for deck and engine department

- Records of drills and emergency responses for DP

- Data logging including faults for the DP system

- Biodata of DP personnel including vessel specific experience

- Familiarisation of DP personnel carried out onboard and their qualification

42. As per MTS/IMCA guidelines where a DP class 2 vessel can be deployed?

As per the IMCA/MTS operations guidance, a DP class 2 vessel may be deployed for the following tasks.

- Shuttle Tanker

- Cable layer/pipe layer

- Diving support

- Drilling

- Heavy Lift

- ROV

- FPSO

- Well stimulation

- Logistics jobs

These are just recommendations. You may come across a vessel carrying out ROV operations, classed as DP 1, in open waters.

43. Where do we use "Heavy Lift" mode in DP vessels?

Heavy lift mode is used onboard crane vessels capable of lifting heavy loads. This take care of the changes while transferring heavy loads and its effects on the DP vessel.

44. Where is "External Force Compensation" mode of DP used?

The external force compensation mode is used normally onboard DP pipe lay barges to take care of the pipe tensions and its effects on the position keeping capabilities of the vessel.

45. Where is "Fire Monitor Compensation" mode of DP used?

Fire monitor compensation mode is used when the vessel is dealing with the different forces related to the fire monitors. The water jets create a big force that needs to be compensated for maintaining the vessels position.

46. What is weathervane mode of DP?

The weathervane mode is used for offshore loading operations. In this mode the vessel is free to rotate and align her heading into the weather. It is a common practice for the FPSO/shuttle tankers that neither their position nor heading is required to be fixed. These vessels follow a circle which is around the loading point.

47. Where target follow or sub follow mode is used in DP applications?

Target follow mode helps the DP vessel to follow an underwater moving target (usually a ROV). The DP system will make use of hydroacoustic position reference sensor for this purpose.

48. What is the "Standby Mode" of a DP System?

In standby mode, the DP system is in reset mode/ preparation mode. While the DP system is in standby mode, there is no output generated by the DP controller. Also, if the DP system is working in any other operational mode, by bringing the system to standby mode, the system can be reset.

49. What is "Joystick Mode" in DP Operations?

While in joystick mode the set points or command for the thrusters is generated by using the joystick lever. The controller of Joystick, based on the movements of the joystick, will generate the set point/command for the required thrusters.

50. Describe the "follow sub mode" or "follow target mode" in DP operations?

While the DP system is using follow sub mode or Follow Target mode, the vessel will follow a target submerged in water, usually the remotely operated vehicle (ROV). While in this mode of operations the position reference used will include hydro acoustic position reference system (HPR) or high precision acoustic positioning (HiPap).

51. Explain what is "Auto Position mode", "DP Mode" or "Auto DP Mode"?

    While the DP system is operating in Auto DP Mode/DP Mode/Auto Position Mode, the set points are generated by the DP controller based on the setting carried out by the DP operator. In this mode all three movements i.e. surge, sway and yaw are controlled automatically.

52. What is "Track Follow" or "Auto track" mode of DP operations?

    While operating in auto track/track follow mode, the vessel follows a pre-determined set of track/s and pre-defined heading. The heading of the vessel can be changed during this process. This mode of operation is generally used for cable laying/pipe laying operations.

53. What is "Mixed Mode" in DP Operations?

    While the vessel operates in "Mixed Mode", the controlled degrees of freedom are controlled in a mixed way, as required by operational requirements. For an example if we keep the heading control by joystick and the surge and the sway can be controlled automatically, this is an example to mixed mode.

54. What may be the source/s of hazard while carrying out diving operations from a DP vessel?

    The vessel is maintained in auto DP mode for the diving operations by using its thrusters. The continuously running thrusters are a potential hazard for divers & umbilical cord of the divers. But this drawback is overcome by the safety standards provided by the DP system.

55. Why is it necessary that the DP Operator must be familiar with the details of the work site?

Before starting DP operations, it is important that the DP operator, carries out a complete hazard identification and risk analysis. For this it is important that the planning includes the needs to identify escape route, blow on and blow off zones.

56. Explain 'Weathervane' or 'Auto Heading Select' mode of operation. When is it used?

This mode is an essential function in shuttle tanker and FPSO type of operations. This mode is particularly used for offtake/offshore loading/shuttle tanker- FPSO operations. Emphasis is on maintaining the position by the shuttle tanker with respect to the FPSO, ensuring safe distances as agreed. The heading keeps changing in the to the weather as per the settings of the "weather wane" mode.

57. Every time the vessel goes into DP mode or auto DP Mode or auto position mode, the engines/generators experience high load and then after some time it may settle down. Is this Normal?

No, it is not normal. The DP operator must endure that the speed and the rate of turn, if the vessel has been on the move, is brought down to generally accepted minimum levels. The speed is expected to be below.5 knot and the rate of turn should be less than 10 degrees per minute. If the vessel is now put on DP, it is very unlikely that the load will shoot up. Bringing the speed and rate of turn down before putting the vessel on DP are part of the good practices.

58. Name one disadvantage of a ship (utilizing its DP system) compared to using anchors while working?

    The major disadvantage is the continually running thrusters which are must for a vessel on DP. These continuously running thrusters may pause hazards for divers and ROVs working underwater.

59. On a DP enabled vessel on Auto DP/Auto Position mode, various alarms/warnings such as Insufficient thrust, heading out of limits, position out of limits and reduced thruster capability are observed. What may be cause of these?

    These alarms/warnings may appear when the thrust is not enough to hold the vessel in its desired position/heading. If all thrusters are online and working well, it may be that the vessel has already reached its limits of operation. DPO must looks at the capability plot and take a decision accordingly. If there is a standby thruster/s these must be enabled now by the DPO to take control of the situation.

60. While on auto position mode, suddenly the DP system rejects all position reference sensors and there is a position drop out alarm. What may be the reason/s?

    All position reference sensors being rejected at a time may be due to a common cause. One of the common causes may be inputs of gyro compass to the position reference sensors have failed. It is recommended to check the gyro distribution panel and fix up the problem.

61. What are the main features of DP familiarisation Checklist?

    This check list specifically pertains to the DP master/ SDPO/DPO/Jr DPOs on joining a DP vessel. The check list must contain familiarisation of the ship's DP equipment and procedures. All DPOS must also be familiarized with the ships bridge equipment.

For the ER watch keepers (including the chief engineer and ETOs the familiarisation check list must include engine room standing instructions for normal and emergency operations. The setting up of the machinery for normal DP operations, being aware of the FMEA and other trials of the vessel is an integral part of the engineer's familiarisation.

62. What are the main features of ECR DP Six Hourly Watchkeeping Checklist?

THE ECR six hourly watchkeeping checklist may include the following so that incoming ER watchkeeper is kept fully updated of the status of ER machinery.

- Power and thruster status

- Bus tie Status

- Cooling water/sea chest

- Battery/UPS/control power supply status

- Compressed air status

- Lubricating oil system status

- Temperature and pressure reading of the various machineries such as thruster, generators etc.

- All required checks and tests on the machinery carried out and found satisfactory.

- The bridge must be kept updated about the above.

63. What are the main features of Vessel on DP and 500-meter Entry Checklist?

When the vessel is set up on "DP Mode/Auto DP Mode/Auto Position Mode", a check list is to be completed by the DP watch keeper. The check list may include the following.

- Client

- Location

- Wok details

- Weather details

- PTW

- Any special work permission such as hot work

- ER check list completed

- Number of equipment available and good working order. This includes the environmental sensors, position reference sensors, generators, thruster and any to the special equipment needed for the operations.

- Vessel controls such as gain level, alarm details, alarm printer status, tests of communications etc.

64. What are the main features of DP operations Pre Set up Checklist for Bridge?

Pre setup check list for conducting DP operations may include all those checks considered necessary for safe operations. Knowing the status of main propulsion, thrusters, power, power management is very important. Equally important is power back up. UPS status, where the thruster controls selected.

The DPO must know which operator station, DP controller are in commend and which all sensors, position reference sensors and other sensors are in use and standby. To continuously monitor the DP system, the DP operator must check if the consequence analysis has been activated and the required DP class(suitable and agreed for the operations) have been selected, alarm printer have been checked and ensure working properly, cleared all existing alarms, details about the environment and the changes expected (weather forecast). It is a good industry practice that the pre-DP check list to be signed by both the DP operators.

65. What are the main features of DP Operations Pre Set Up Checklist for Engine Room?

The engine room must be preparing well before the starting of the DP operations. The ER watch keeper must check that alarms in the ER are taken care of and no vital alarms present. Carefully knowing the status of fuel oil system, lube oil system, sea water and freshwater cooling system are working well, and all parameters are with in normal limits.

The duty engineer must also check and record the status of power and power management system,, the generators online and standby, the reserve power and limitations, status of water tight doors for ensuring redundancy pf the DP class and agreed for the operations. The status of the bus tie breakers and the requirement for the current operations must be checked and recorded.

66. What are the main features of DP Hand Over Checklist?

The DP hand over check list may include lots of information so that the incoming DP operator is fully aware about the

DP system and the current status. The DP hand over check list may include the following.

- Date/time

- Location

- Client

- Present position

- Weather conditions and forecast

- Use of position reference sensors and any restrictions

- Thrusters and their status

- Generators and their status

- Sensors/PRS and their status

- DP settings/Joystick settings/IJS settings

- Communications set up with various locations

Date

Date	
Location	
Working With	
Client	

Before Going on DP

Before Going on DP	
Side to be Worked	☐
Installation Heading Noted	☐
Sufficient Generators on each side of Switchboard	☐
Required Thrusters Started	☐
Weather Forecast OK	☐
Current/Tides Evaluated	☐
Printer Online/Paper Supply Checked	☐
Aft Console Controls Checked	☐
Backup Joystick Online	☐

Once Vessel Is On DP

Once Vessel Is On DP			
Mode Selected		JOY	DP
DP OS in Command	OS1	OS2	OS3
DP CC in Command	CC1	CC2	CC3
Engine Room Informed on DP			☐
ER DP Setup Checklist Completed			☐
500m Checklist Complete			☐
Marine Installation Informed			☐
DP Class 2 Selected			☐
Equipment in the Water			
Draft (Max)			m
Time on DP/Take Over Watch			

Outgoing DPO signature	Incoming DPO signature
Name	Name

Present Position

Present Position	
Northings/Latitude	
Eastings/Longitude	

Environment

Environment					
Wind	Dir	˚	Speed		knts
Current	Dir	˚	Speed		knts
Swell	Ht				mtrs

Thrusters

Thrusters	BT1	BT2	ST1	Port AZI/ CPP	Stbd AZI/ CPP	Rudder P & S
Online	☐	☐	☐	☐	☐	☐
Setpoint/ Feedback	☐	☐	☐	☐	☐	☐
Main Prop & Rudder Mode						
Rudder Gain						%
Stern Thruster Gain		Azi/Main First		Equal		Tunnel First

Generators & PMS

Generators & PMS	Shaft Gen (P)	Shaft Gen (S)	Auxiliary
Online	☐	☐	☐
Bus Tie	Open		Closed

Power

Power		
Available	kW	kW
Used	kW	kW

Joystick Settings

Joystick Settings			
Joystick Sensitivity	Low		High
Joystick Response	Linear		Progressive
Pivot Centre	Fore	Centre	Aft

Position Reference Systems

Position Reference Systems				
DGPS 1	Diff Data =		HDOP =	
	Weight =	%	Primary	Secondary
DGPS 2	Diff Data =		HDOP =	
	Weight =	%	Primary	Secondary
Cyscan	Target Range =	m	Bearing =	˚
	Weight =	%	Primary	Secondary
Any Other PRS :				

Sensors

Sensors							
Gyro	Direction	Anem	Speed	Direction	VRU	Roll	Pitch
1	˚	1	kts	˚	1	˚	˚
2	˚	2	kts	˚	2	˚	˚
3	˚	3	kts	˚	3	˚	˚
	Primary			Secondary		Filter Value	
Gyro							
Anemometer							
VRU							

DP Settings

DP Settings	Heading			Position		
Alarms	W =	˚	A=	˚	W =	m A= m
Settings	Position =		Velocity =		Integral =	
Priority	Heading			Position		
OP Centre			ROT			˚/min

Communications

Communications				
Deck Ch	VHF	WT	ROV Coms	
Engine Room Ch	VHF	WT	Survey Coms	
Installation Ch	VHF	WT	Ships Phone	
Crane Ch	VHF	WT		

Fig 15.4 DP Hand Over Check List (Courtesy Wintermar)

67. What are the main features of DP Set up Checklist?

    The DP setup check list prepared for the bridge may include the following ensuring safe operations.

    - Date, Time, Location

    - DP Mode, systems in Use (OS and PS)

    - Measurement/Engineering units (metric/User Defined etc.)

68. What are the main features of Engine Room check list for DP?

    The engine room check list for DP generally includes most of the other checks as suggested in the other ER check lists except the specific checks for particular tasks. The general checklist must include the fuel oil tanks, drainage of water contents, cooling arrangements and status, lube oil system, all thruster and propulsion system, power and power management including UPS and status of bus tie breakers. The HVAC system must also be checked for optimal operations. On completion of the check list, the same must be signed by the duty engineers with remarks if required and the same must be reported to the bridge.

DP BRIDGE 6 Hourly Watch Keeping Checklist

DATE:	TIME:	LOCATION:	CLIENT:

MODE SELECTION

Standby ☐   Joystick ☐   DP ☐   Follow Target ☐

SYSTEM

CONTROLLER STATUS: DP PS01 ☐   DP PS11 ☐

TIME SETTINGS: Zone Time

ENGINEERING UNITS: Metric ☐   Imperial ☐   User Defined 1 ☐   User Defined 2 ☐

COORDINATE SYSTEM: WGS 84 ☐   UTM ☐

COMMAND CONTROL: OS 1 ☐   OS 2 ☐

SETTINGS

THRUSTER: Bow 1 ☐   Bow 2 ☐   Stern 1 ☐

ENGINE: Port Main ☐   Stbd Main ☐

RUDDER: Port ☐   Stbd ☐

THRUSTER ALLOCATION: Rudder Inwards ☐   Rudder Outwards ☐   Port Main Fwd ☐   Stbd Main Fwd ☐

RUDDER GAIN: Min ☐   Equal ☐   Max ☐

TUNNEL THRUSTER: Main ☐   Equal ☐   Tunnel ☐

VESSEL RESPONSE SETTING: Change Sensitivity .... Velocity .... Integral ....

CHANGE PRIORITY: Heading ☐   Position ☐

JOYSTICK - SENSITIVITY: Low ☐   High ☐

    - RESPONSE: Linear ☐   Progressive ☐

    - PIVOT CENTRE: Fore ☐   Centre ☐   Aft ☐

POWER

GENERATORS ONLINE: SG 1 ☐   SG 2 ☐   Aux 1 ☐   Aux 2 ☐

BUS TIES: A~B Open ☐ Closed ☐   A~C Open ☐ Closed ☐   C~D Open ☐ Closed ☐

POWER	Bus 1 Available .... kW	Bus 2 Available .... kW	
	Bus 1 Used .... kW	Bus 2 Used .... kW	

SENSOR

DGPS 1 ☐   DGPS 2 ☐   HPR ☐   RADIUS ☐

DP BRIDGE 6 Hourly Watch Keeping Checklist

Gyro 1 ☐ Gyro 2 ☐ Gyro 3 ☐	Wind 1 ☐ Wind 2 ☐ Wind 3 ☐
VRU 1 ☐ VRU 2 ☐ VRU 3 ☐	Speed 1 ☐ Speed 2 ☐
ROT 1 ☐ ROT 2 ☐	

REFERENCE SYSTEM SETUP: DGPS 1

GPS Diff ☐   Satellites : 4 ☐   HDOP : 4 ☐   Age Of Diff Signal : 60 ☐   Action Setup : Warning ☐   Reject ☐

REFERENCE SYSTEM PHILOSOPHY: Primary / Secondary ☐   Weighting ☐

Filter: Low ☐   Normal ☐   High ☐

REFERENCE SYSTEM SETUP: DGPS 2

GPS Diff ☐   Satellites : 4 ☐   HDOP : 4 ☐   Age Of Diff Signal : 60 ☐   Action Setup : Warning ☐   Reject ☐

REFERENCE SYSTEM PHILOSOPHY: Primary / Secondary ☐   Weighting ☐

Filter: Low ☐   Normal ☐   High ☐

DP

HEADING MOVE: Shortest ☐   ROT .... °/min

POSITION MOVE: Speed .... knots

ALARM LIMITS: Heading Warn ....° Alarm ....°
Position Warn ....m Alarm ....m

ALARM SETUP: Enable Alarm Printing ☐

CONSEQUENCE ANALYSIS: DP Class 2 ☐

Position .... N .... E	Heading ....°	Wind ....° .... kts	Current ....° .... kts

FUGRO DGPS

DGPS 1: HIGH ☐ LOW ☐   Signal Strength .... dB

DGPS 2: HIGH ☐ LOW ☐   Signal Strength .... dB

CYSCAN / RADIUS / FANBEAM / MINIRADA

Brightness: Range: Bearing:

Name & Rank .... Signature ....

Name & Rank .... Signature ....

Fig:15.5   DP Six Hourly Check List (Bridge) - (Courtesy Wintermar)

69. What are the main features of DP station keeping Incident form?

DP station keeping incident form must be completed by the responsible person onboard and sent to the DP manager/ DPA and if agreed must also be shared with the IMCA as per the industry practice. The information in a standard incident reporting form may include the following.

- Any situation which may have led to a "Red Alert"

- Any "undesired event".

- DP down time if any.

- Issues and problems with position keeping restrictions which forced the vessel to come out of operational status and go in for an investigation/rectification of problem/ breakdown or trials after fixing the problem.

70. What are the main features of Off-DP/Post DP Checklist?

The post DP/Off DP check list to ensure that the DP system is, and related machinery is taken care of accordingly. All sensors/PRS are taken off/retrieved safely and secured as per the guidelines. If the vessel is moving to the next location ensuring that the auto pilot of sailing settings are made accordingly. A sample of the off DP/Post DP Checklist is given below.

Post DP Checklist	
Client informed (time):	
Green light OFF:	
Installation informed intention to come off D.P:	
Engine room informed (coming off D.P.):	
ROV / Divers informed:	
Galley informed (*if required*):	
All overboard lines recovered:	
HPR pole up - gate valve closed.(if required):	
RADius 1000 reflector recovered:	
RAM. (restricted in ability to maneuver) lights off & shapes down:	
Vessel off AUTO D.P. (time):	
Cranes stowed:	
Vessel made secure for sea passage: (*inc clients equipment*)	
Thruster fans stopped and vents closed as required:	
Check autopilot settings:	
Signed:	(DPO)
Date/Time:	

Fig: 15.6   Example - Off DP/Post DP Check List (Courtesy Wintermar)

www.ingramcontent.com/pod-product-compliance
Lightning Source LLC
Chambersburg PA
CBHW021137260726
48656CB00023B/176